# TRUTH

MARK FALLON-CYR, M.D.

Truth
Copyright © 2024 by Mark Fallon-Cyr, M.D.

All rights reserved. No part of this publication may be reproduced, distributed, or transmitted in any form or by any means, including photocopying, recording or other electronic or mechanical methods, without the prior written permission of the author, except in the case of brief quotations embodied in reviews and certain other non-commercial uses permitted by copyright law.

Without in any way limiting the author's and publisher's exclusive rights under copyright, any use of this publication to "train" generative artificial intelligence (AI) technologies to generate text is expressly prohibited. The author reserves all rights to license uses of this work for generative AI training and development of machine learning language models.

NO AI TRAINING: Without in any way limiting the author's [and publisher's] exclusive rights under copyright, any use of this publication to "train" generative artificial intelligence (AI) technologies to generate text is expressly prohibited. The author reserves all rights to license uses of this work for generative AI training and development of machine learning language models.

Printed in the United States of America

Hardcover: 979-8-9893832-5-2
Paperback: 979-8-9893832-4-5
Ebook ISBN: 979-8-9893832-2-1

True Success Press
Durango, Colorado

*Dedicated to all who advocate for the truth.*

# Table of Contents

SECTION ONE: The Importance of Truth . . . . . . . . . . . . . . . 1

The Importance of Truth. . . . . . . . . . . . . . . . . . . . . . . 3

SECTION TWO: A Framework for Understanding Truth. . . . . . 17

A Framework for Understanding Truth . . . . . . . . . . . . . . . 19

Truth . . . . . . . . . . . . . . . . . . . . . . . . . . . . . . . . . 21

Objective Universal Truth . . . . . . . . . . . . . . . . . . . . . . 23

Falsehoods . . . . . . . . . . . . . . . . . . . . . . . . . . . . . . 25

Partial Truths . . . . . . . . . . . . . . . . . . . . . . . . . . . . 29

The Whole Truth . . . . . . . . . . . . . . . . . . . . . . . . . . 33

Unknowns . . . . . . . . . . . . . . . . . . . . . . . . . . . . . . 35

Metaphors . . . . . . . . . . . . . . . . . . . . . . . . . . . . . . 37

Fiction and Fantasy . . . . . . . . . . . . . . . . . . . . . . . . . 39

Ideas . . . . . . . . . . . . . . . . . . . . . . . . . . . . . . . . . 41

Concepts . . . . . . . . . . . . . . . . . . . . . . . . . . . . . . . 45

Beliefs and Meanings . . . . . . . . . . . . . . . . . . . . . . . . 49

Intuitions . . . . . . . . . . . . . . . . . . . . . . . . . . . . . . . 55

Social Constructs . . . . . . . . . . . . . . . . . . . . . . . . . . 57

Mixtures and Combinations . . . . . . . . . . . . . . . . . . . . 63

Personal Truth. . . . . . . . . . . . . . . . . . . . . . . . . . . . .65
Summary. . . . . . . . . . . . . . . . . . . . . . . . . . . . . . . . .69

SECTION THREE: Working With Truth. . . . . . . . . . . . . . .71
Working With Truth . . . . . . . . . . . . . . . . . . . . . . . . . . . .73
Our Relationship With the Truth. . . . . . . . . . . . . . . . . . . .75
How Truth is Determined . . . . . . . . . . . . . . . . . . . . . . . .77
Cognitive Skills That Support
Our Investigation . . . . . . . . . . . . . . . . . . . . . . . . . . . . .81
Degree of Certainty. . . . . . . . . . . . . . . . . . . . . . . . . . . .87
Truthful Communication . . . . . . . . . . . . . . . . . . . . . . . .91
Final Thoughts on Truth . . . . . . . . . . . . . . . . . . . . . . . .95
Acknowledgements . . . . . . . . . . . . . . . . . . . . . . . . . . . .99
Appendix: Categories of Experience as They Relate to Truth . . . . 101
Bibliography . . . . . . . . . . . . . . . . . . . . . . . . . . . . . . . 105
About the Author . . . . . . . . . . . . . . . . . . . . . . . . . . . . 107

# Section One

# The Importance of Truth

# The Importance of Truth

In today's world, we are suffering a breakdown of Truth. These days, it is not uncommon to see hostilities arise as different groups champion their "truth" to the world. The comment sections on social media are rife with caustic, untruthful remarks. Many news organizations distort facts in order to promote financial and political agendas. And AI-generated memes and videos flood our screens with false narratives that distort the truth as people attempt to manipulate our feelings and opinions about world events. Given the widespread prevalence of falsehoods and their negative impact on our world, I feel inspired to offer some reflections that can strengthen our footing when we are searching for truth. I believe that a clear foundation in truth is essential if we hope to support healthy growth and development for humanity.

When I told a good friend of mine that I was going to write a short book on truth, he initially tried to discourage me. He told me that most people are not interested in "academic topics," for they're more interested in issues that are relevant to their own lives. This surprised me because I believe that there are few things as personally and socially relevant to us as *truth*. If we want to understand ourselves, others, and important issues in our world, we need to know what is true, what is factual, and what is actually unfolding in the world. Truth is the foundation of vibrant, successful living. Without dependable, solid information on which to build our dreams, livelihoods, and communities, our structures crumble. Truth is not an academic topic; it is a cornerstone of successful living.

When we are living in the midst of untruths and falsehoods, we experience a lot of chaos. Without accurate information, it's easy to head in the wrong direction or get lost; it's impossible to resolve our problems or arrive at the right conclusions; and it's hard to plan and strategize effectively. In an absence of truth (or a distortion of truth) our projects suffer, our dreams can't get off the ground, and we can't make effective decisions, and sometimes, there is incredible harm. When mistruths are propagated, it can bring us into collision with others and the world: wars are fought, governments fall, marriages collapse, friendships end, communities divide, people are subjugated, livelihoods are stolen, and families are torn apart. The spread of untruths targeting specific people, cultures, and events has resulted in widespread abuses leading to oppression, racism, and genocide. When untruths abound – whether through fabrications, falsehoods, misunderstandings, lies, or delusions – they bring chaos and destruction to individuals, communities, and global structures.

If we wish to elevate the condition of humanity, we must build a foundation of truth. We need to get to the heart of truth, know what it is, learn how to identify it, recognize when it is being suppressed, and work diligently to cultivate truth for the success of our world.

## Chasing Down Truth

In my own quest to understand truth, I reviewed numerous books and articles on the subject and quickly realized why my friend had been so cautious in advising me about writing a treatise on truth. In Western literature, truth is often treated as an academic pursuit – the writing is often confusing and convoluted, and many discourses are filled with complex words and dense "heady" explanations. To be clear, I hold a degree in medicine, and I struggled to understand what they were talking about. In the end, much of what I found did not feel helpful or relevant to my own life. For example, one writer wrote:

> *"... the fact that truth is a 'thin' concept does not imply that it does not carry with it certain constitutive commitments. In this sense, I want to argue, our ordinary notion of truth involves the idea that it is a norm of enquiry, and that the rejection of this normative character, wherever it comes from, threatens the very coherence of our theoretical endeavours. Now it might be objected that this threat is just the one that many sceptical or nihilistic contemporary conceptions let hang over our most serious rationalistic enterprises. To answer it, we do not only need to analyse our ordinary concept of truth, but also to get into an account of truth as a cognitive value."*[1]

This teaching does not help us to understand truth, nor is it particularly useful to our everyday living. It is not useful in navigating our job, our home life, or raising our kids, much less in dealing with important issues that affect our world.

However, a workable understanding of truth is accessible. We can gain clarity about what *is* and *isn't* truth. We can cultivate a clear understanding of its nature and apply it to our everyday lives and the challenges we face in our world. When we are grounded in truth, we are empowered to make healthy, successful choices and take effective action. We may have to use some deep thinking to understand the nuances and intricacies of truth, but doing so will foster a strong foundation in knowing what truth is, and how best to work with it.

As I was contemplating this need for "deep thinking" to uncover truth, another good friend reminded me of a quote by the philosopher Don Marquis: "If you make people think they're thinking, they'll love you. If you really make them think, they'll hate you." I believe there's some truth to this statement. As a society, we tend to shy away from deep reflection. Today, we see many social messages promoting the idea that deep thinking is not cool – that it should in fact, be avoided. Media feeds offer up short sound bites,

---

[1] Engel, Pascal. "Truth." *Central Problems of Philosophy*, edited by John Shand, McGill-Queens University Press, 2002.

brimming with catchy headlines and tantalizing images that encourage mindless scrolling behavior. When you do engage with the content, it often offers "quick fixes" for our problems; we don't need to work hard for our success, we just need to practice the influencer's handy tips. This orientation does not invite us to pursue deep thinking. But it is our human nature to think deeply. In fact, most of us enjoy thinking deeply about the things that we care about. Wouldn't you love to sit down and have a deep discussion with someone about an issue that's dear to your heart? When we exchange ideas and philosophies, our interest and curiosity awakens and our mind expands in ways that feel stimulating and exciting.

Deep thinking incorporates qualities that help us *get to the bottom of things*. It builds strong cognitive skills that strengthen our mental capacities. When we are engaged in deep thinking, we are observant and compare differences; we weigh the pros and cons of a situation; we excavate and take apart ideas and concepts; and we develop our intuitive skills. Deep thinking also requires a willingness to form independent conclusions, even when they differ from the collective beliefs of those around us. When we cultivate our capacity for deep thinking, we are able to discern what is truthful, what is obscured or "fuzzy" truth, and what is outright manipulation.

I invite you to embrace your own capacity for deep reflection. As you open your mind to deep thinking, I believe you'll feel more alive and engaged with life. You'll begin to touch into a deeper wisdom within you that offers strength and clarity, enabling you to more readily fulfill your passions, dreams, and desires. With enough practice, deep thinking will feel quite natural to you and serve as a useful tool in creating the life you've dreamed of.

With this in mind, let's take a moment to practice some deep thinking with a reflection on truth, for anytime we contemplate new ideas, it can be useful to reflect and examine our own values, beliefs, and conditioning as they relate to the material at hand. Throughout this book, I offer reflections that will deepen your understanding of truth and the role it plays in your life. I invite you to check out the exercise below.

## Assessing Your Understanding of Truth

To begin, take a moment to relax, breathing out any tension you notice – stressful feelings, sensations, or thoughts that are making you uncomfortable. Imagine that you can gently breathe out these tensions with each out-breath. When you feel more relaxed and settled, read the following questions, and notice what responses arise in you. If you like, you can write down your answers. If any of the questions seem confusing or difficult for you, simply be aware of what is arising and note your response. Sometimes, it takes a little practice to awaken our deep thinking.

*How do you define *truth*?

*What role does truth play in your life? Is it important and prominent, or does it take on a lesser role?

*How important is it to be truthful to yourself? Is it important to tell yourself the truth, or do you tend to "smooth things over" as you talk to yourself about difficult subjects?

*Are there certain areas of your life where it's hard to tell yourself the truth, or hard to accept the truth? Perhaps you struggle to be truthful about unhealthy habits, an addiction, or a problem in a relationship. If so, how does it make you feel when you avoid the truth in this area? What impact does that have on your life?

*What role does truth play with your family and friends? Are you truthful in your communication with them? Do you believe that they communicate truthfully to you?

*How do you see truth expressed or not expressed in our world?

Do you wish the world was more truthful?

*Do you think it's possible to know the truth in this world?

I believe that it's important to think deeply about truth for it is a cornerstone of healthy living. To create a successful world, we need both personal and collective accountability in pursuing and advocating for the truth, for truth offers the information we need to build a healthy, fair, and equitable world. If we don't take responsibility for understanding and advocating truth, who else is going to do it?

## Our Confusion about Truth

In our current culture, there is tremendous confusion about the concept of truth. These days, there is such a strong breakdown in our understanding of truth, people actually argue about what truth is! We hear phrases like, "Well, that might be *your* truth, but it isn't *my* truth!" We are unable to agree on a set definition of truth. How did we get so confused? Many factors contribute to our confusion. Let's identify a few that are particularly significant.

One contributing factor pertains to the way media is used in our culture. In many arenas, media is employed to distort information and "rework" the truth. When news organizations, corporations, political groups, and marketers want to influence the masses in their favor, they can employ a variety of techniques to manipulate the truth: They may skew data reports; photoshop or alter images; hyper-focus on stories that are emotionally charged to draw attention from more important stories; they may craft eye-catching headlines and sound bites to misrepresent a story. Have you ever read a newspaper article with an attention-getting headline, only to find that the main ideas and meaning of the story were completely different from what the headline led you to believe? Have you seen photos in the media that sparked strong emotions in you, only to realize that they were used completely out of context? When our media is engineered to deceive, it becomes harder to trust our eyes and ears, leading to great confusion and chaos.

Sadly, with the advances in AI and technology, media manipulation is on the rise and soon it will be hard to detect fictionalized representations. Since we can't always rely on our media to tell us the truth, it's important for us to take responsibility in learning how to identify and eliminate fabrications from our media feeds. We need to become astute detectives, so we can better recognize media manipulation and its effects on our mind, body, and heart. For an introduction to this education, you can watch the documentary, *The Social Dilemma*. It offers important information on how the media is influencing our greater society.

A second factor contributing to our confusion about the truth lies in the fact that our current education models do not focus enough on Truth, Ethics, and Critical Thinking. Deep thinking and reflective skills need to be taught and cultivated in order to flourish. When we are not skilled in deep thinking, we can be easily duped by others' agendas and manipulations, especially when they come in sparkly, enticing packaging that is meant to distract us. For example, if you do not understand the concept of "rhetoric" (ways of using language persuasively) you might be taken in by another's flowery language when they are, in fact, offering something harmful: A politician may talk about "job creation" while promoting a new factory (that he has a personal or financial stake in), leaving out information on how polluting the factory will be for the community. When we are untrained in critical thinking skills, it is hard to discern nuances in the realm of truth, morality, and the art of manipulation.

Another factor that causes confusion about truth is our lack of understanding on how psychological beliefs impact our "version" of the truth. Our psychology – one factor in how we see and interpret the world – is built on personal meanings, social concepts, and cultural beliefs that inform our worldview. Our perceptions and psychological beliefs greatly influence what we think truth is, and those beliefs go on to influence our actions, our choices, and our behaviors. For instance, if you believe that the world is a safe place, you are more likely to have faith in the trustworthiness of others. But if you believe that the world is full of treacherous people, you'll likely be suspicious of everyone – unable to trust the truth, even when it is offered by an honest and scrupulous person.

A potent example of how psychology impacts our understanding of truth can be found in the debate over vaccines. Across the world, people carry different beliefs about the impacts of vaccines on our health and body. Some see vaccines as a health benefit that protects us, while others see them as an invasive agent that harms us or even controls us, infringing on our personal liberties. What is interesting about this dilemma is that *both sides* believe that they are holding the "truth" on this matter. But as we'll come to see in our explorations, there is a distinct difference between *beliefs* and *truth*, and knowing the difference can empower us to make effective choices.

When we are suffering from afflicted psychology, or our mind is consumed with fears and painful beliefs, we are less likely to be interested in the truth, and we are more likely to adhere to what we believe are self-preserving behaviors. When people are stuck in "survival mode" they can knowingly perpetuate falsehoods, believing that they must manipulate others to get their needs met. In these instances, they may carry a misguided sense of right and wrong, justifying their manipulations in order to get more money, attention, status, or power. In my years as a psychiatrist, I have seen that those who manipulate the truth for their own gain, do so out of fear, woundedness, or ignorance. Personally, I do not believe that deceptive behavior is inherent in our human nature; it is a result of fear, pain, and trauma. Luckily, when we do the inner work to heal ourselves and release our fears, we naturally return to a foundation of more truthful living.

> Deception is not inherent to our human nature; it arises out of fear, pain and trauma.

Another factor that contributes to our confusion about the truth lies in our lack of knowledge. Sometimes, people unknowingly distort the truth because they simply don't know any better. In their hearts, they believe that they're telling the truth, when in fact, they lack information, or they have a limited view of the world. This often happens when we are uneducated about a subject and form opinions on it based on our limited knowledge: We may honestly believe that we know what a political figure stands for, based on the comments made by our family and friends, never suspecting that we are misinformed. We are giving our honest opinion, but our viewpoint isn't based on facts.

Confusion about the truth can also be influenced by aversive and traumatic experiences. If you grew up in a war zone and your community was bombed by the United States military, you may believe that it's truthful to say, "All Americans are bad." While this may be your honest, personal viewpoint, it is not the truth about all Americans. Yet this belief may shape your mindstate and actions, especially towards Americans, and you may live a life oriented toward vengeance and retaliation. Anytime we lack full information, or we are under duress, the truth can be skewed and distorted within us, bringing much harm and damage.

When the truth is distorted, everyone's health and well-being are compromised. A lack of truth can break down family connections, threaten a community's stability, or bring chaos to the world. Imagine the potential impact when there is a lack of truth concerning a marriage, a substance-abusing partner, or a financial institution. Imagine how misinformation promotes racism or violence. Consider how distorting or withholding the truth can escalate nuclear weapon proliferation, global warming, species extinction, and toxic exposures to our land, food, and water. The practice of deception is detrimental, not only to humans, but the entire world. Add to this, the advent of computers and computer-generated images, and it is now easier to proliferate false information quickly across the planet. It is a well-documented fact that fake videos and misinformation spread virally across the internet much faster than truthful articles. This makes sense since virulent commentary can fuel fear and anger, getting us to tap the "share" button much more readily.

If we wish to create a successful life on this planet, we need to make a conscious effort to highlight all the ways that untruths are contributing to our demise. Falsehoods, distortions, deceptions – *any* lapses in truth – are harmful. They wreak havoc and keep us from manifesting healthy, sustainable living. I believe that once we make the effort to promote truthful information in our affairs, we will lay a path to healthier living and a brighter future for all.

## The Benefits of Aligning with Truth

When we align ourselves with truth, we stand on solid, stable ground. Long-term success requires a stable foundation. One of the reasons why truth is so valuable is because it stands the test of time. It is not variable. It does not change with humanity's whims and beliefs. For instance, there was a time when humans believed that illnesses were due to "evil spirits." But it has always been true that germs play a role in sickness, whether we were aware of it or not. Earlier in our history, humans believed that the universe was made up of only four elements – earth, water, fire, and air. The truth is *many elements* (carbon, hydrogen, iron, etc.) blend and ignite together to create our universe. Falsehoods always break down over time. Our knowledge of the world may change, our beliefs may change, but truth remains, offering a stable means for creating an informed, well-constructed life. It behooves us to seek out the truth for it will never let us down.

> Long-term success is built on the reliability and stability of truth.

When we invest in the truth, there are great personal benefits to be gained. Aligned with truth, we possess information that helps us develop into healthy, happy, *authentic* individuals. When we tell the truth to ourselves – about our eating, our exercise patterns, our habits, and our shortcomings – we step into accountability that encourages us to make better choices around our health and wellbeing. When we tell the truth about our passions, wishes, and aspirations, we lay a path to unfolding our True Nature, that which expresses our deepest heart and desires. When we listen to our deep inner wisdom – insights offered up by our True Nature – it serves as an inner compass, pointing "True North" toward the fulfillment of a meaningful life. And when we embrace truth in our personal relationships, we create healthy, supportive interactions, fostering meaningful connections with friends, co-workers, and loved ones. Living with truth empowers us to meet life in all its complexity: we are better equipped to deal with others; we can understand real consequences in the world; and we can solve problems and make informed decisions, strategizing and inventing new solutions that can carry us toward a successful future. A foundation in truth gets us closer to who we are meant to be.

When we invest in truth on a societal level, we benefit tremendously. Seeing the truth of things, we may realize that we need to invest in our communities – we may need to build up our infrastructure, safety, community connections, or education – all to the benefit of our citizens. Our pursuits of truth in the past have birthed incredible developments and achievements across our world. Truth supports our scientific, mathematical, and technological development, allowing us to achieve incredible feats and build amazing inventions. We have created computers, electric cars, and MRI machines. We've sent satellites into space that allow us to talk face-to-face with someone across the world. And we can now study illnesses at a micro-level, allowing us to treat and eradicate diseases, bringing greater quality of life and longer life expectancy. Our communal pursuit of truth has benefited humankind in a myriad of ways.

Finally, when we tell the truth about our social challenges – poverty, racism, and inequities in healthcare, education, wealth, and the workplace – we gain awareness and knowledge that allows us to improve the human condition. Back in the early twentieth century, journalists, photographers, and writers began documenting the truths about the appalling working conditions endured by men, women, and children in American factories. Through this "truth-telling," the country was inspired to make significant changes that benefited all American workers. Today's standards of employment – an eight-hour workday, paid sick leave, vacation time, and safety protocols – all emerged due to truth-telling about our work environments. This would never have happened without acknowledging the truth of the heinous conditions endured by those factory workers.

Oftentimes, truth-telling demands that we grow a strong "backbone" so we can bear witness to difficult conditions. When we foster a passion for truth, we grow the muscle it takes to create a healthier, better world.

## Valuing Truth

In my work as a psychiatrist, I have come to believe that it is in our human nature to value truth and be truthful. None of us want to be deceived or misled. We want to be able to trust our companions, secure in the knowledge that they will act truthfully and with integrity. We are all born with an innate potential and drive to seek out the truth, and we are wired to sense when something is truthful or not. But our capacity to work with truth needs to be cultivated. Learning is a two-way street: We can be conditioned in healthy ways that strengthen our understanding and connection to truth, or we can be conditioned in harmful ways that hinder our ability to track and recognize truth. Since knowing the truth helps us grow and evolve in healthy ways, it behooves us to teach our children and citizens how to recognize and advance truth in our lives.

## A Collective Vision of Truth

With the belief that truth is endemic to our human nature, I have abundant hope that we can nurture a passion for truth in our world. It may require some deep thinking and a strong backbone, but we can come together to create a clear, *collective vision of truth* that cuts through the deception that plagues our world today. We can unite in a common directive to collectively and collaboratively investigate the truth. We can outline a unified definition of truth and a common language to discuss and quantify truth. And we can commit to collaborating and sharing our knowledge with others to bring healing and peace to the many divisions that exist across our world today. If we make this commitment, we will advance humanity with even yet-to-be-conceived gains benefiting all of humankind, for we are all in this together.

How can we cultivate a rich, shared understanding of truth? We can do this through an exploration of what truth *is* and what truth *isn't*. The first steps involve identifying, examining, and mapping the life experiences that shape our understanding of truth and its place in our lives. In the following section, I will present fifteen categories of experience that are relative to our understanding of truth. As we come to understand the complexities surrounding truth, we will become more proficient at critical thinking, deep thinking, and discerning the truth. This clarity will empower us to dismiss falsehoods that cause chaos and problems, and step onto a new path that leads to healthy, successful, stable living. When we learn to advocate for the truth, we are part of the solution.

> Together, we can create a clear, collective Vision of Truth.

Note: Before we move ahead, I wish to make one clarifying distinction in our exploration of truth. Oftentimes in the English language, we use the word "true" as an adjective – as in *true friend, true love, true hearted,* or *True Nature.* In these examples, we are using the word "true" to describe something as being deeply genuine, authentic, or ideal. In this book, we will be focusing on "true" and "truth" as conforming to fact, actuality, and reality – utilizing our deep thinking to bring a sophisticated, nuanced understanding to the conception of truth and its role in our life.

Section Two

# A Framework for Understanding Truth

# A Framework for Understanding Truth

For millennia, humans have been arguing about truth – debating about "spiritual" truths, "scientific" truths, "personal" truths, and "communal" truths. Delving into a discussion of truth, we quickly find ourselves in a quagmire: Everyone has an opinion on the matter, but is everyone right?

In this section, we offer a framework that gives a clearer understanding of truth. Here, I parcel out, look at, and explore the nature of our experiences as they relate to our perception and understanding of truth. This includes the things we see, hear, think, and say in our everyday life experiences – watching the news, talking with family and friends, listening to a church sermon, cruising the internet, or philosophizing about life. I have organized these experiences into fifteen different categories. These categories of experience do not cover *all* our experiences, we are just focusing on the ones that relate to our understanding of truth.

We may not be consciously aware of these categories, but they greatly impact how we think about and navigate truth-telling. As we become conscious of these categories, we will greatly improve our capacity to discern what truth *is* and *isn't*, thereby increasing our effectiveness as we go through the world.

The fifteen categories are...

1. Truth
2. Objective Universal Truth
3. Falsehoods
4. Partial Truths
5. The "Whole" Truth
6. Unknowns
7. Metaphors
8. Fiction and Fantasy
9. Ideas
10. Concepts
11. Beliefs and Meanings
12. Intuitions
13. Social Constructs
14. Mixtures and Combinations
15. Personal Truth

An examination of truth from these different angles and perspectives can offer us a much richer, more nuanced understanding of what truth actually is and how we might apply our understanding to the complex world around us. When we have a clear understanding of truth, we bring greater clarity and wisdom to our deliberations and actions.

# Truth

Voltaire, an 18th-century philosopher and historian, defined truth as "a statement of the facts as they are." In other words, truth is a *fact*. It is based on reality, corresponding to what actually exists. It is not our ideas or beliefs about things, it is what is real, objective, and factual. If you drop a ball on a calm day, it will fall to the ground; water freezes at 32 degrees Fahrenheit; we need air, water, and food to survive; since we are born, we will die – these are factual truths. Truth is objective – it does not depend upon what anyone believes. Water freezes at 32 degrees, whether you believe it or not. When it comes to truth, the definition is straightforward and clear: It is concerned with the *facts* of the matter.

Truths exist both in the physical world (water freezes at 32 degrees) and in our internal world. For example, it is a fact that we have experiences, thoughts, ideas, beliefs, intuitions, and biases. The existence of these phenomena is an objective fact. However, the content of our beliefs or thoughts may or may not be true. It may be true that you fear monsters under your bed, but it's not necessarily true that there are monsters

> Truth is fact. It is real and objective, based on actual existence.

under your bed. Believing something to be the truth does not make it the truth.

It is also important to clarify that while truths are facts, our *interpretations* of facts may not be true. Imagine that a number of people see a non-distinct light traveling across the night sky. While it is a fact that there was a light moving across the sky, there may be many interpretations and beliefs about that light. Some might say that it's aliens. Some might say that it is a message from God. Others may claim that it is a military exercise. When we are entangled in interpretations, we can get lost in a myriad of theories, none of which may be true. Focusing on facts, gives us stable material to work with.

When we are working with facts, it brings a certain stability to our endeavors. Facts have a predictability to them; they do not waver. They allow us to measure the real relationship between things so we can understand the consequences, implications, and outcomes of those interactions. If you know that "dark heavy clouds" often bring "rain," (a reasonable fact) you can grab your umbrella when you walk out the door to go to work. Facts allow us to make predictions and plan, giving us a solid footing as we go through life pursuing our dreams and aspirations.

Truth is not arbitrary. It is not subject to our whims or our ignorance on matters. Since truth is factual, reliable, and stable, we can trust it and let it guide us.

# Objective Universal Truth

*Objective universal truths* are another facet of truth. They are factual and real, but they exist beyond individual people. Objective universal truths can be experienced by anyone if they have the necessary knowledge, opportunities, and support. People across the world, with the right resources, can investigate an issue and arrive at the same conclusion. For example, if one hundred people scattered across the world have knowledge of astronomy and a good telescope, and they point their telescope at a particular place in the night sky, they will all see the Orion Nebula. In other words, they come to the same conclusion because the existence of the Orion Nebula is a *universal fact*. Objective universal truths are verifiable by anyone with the right resources.

What do I mean by the "right resources?" If you are studying the night sky and you wish to find truths about it, you need certain conditions to discover those truths. You need to have the passion and vision for delving into the unknowns of the heavens. You need appropriate patience and analytical thinking. You need the right environment and tools such as an observatory with a good telescope to track the movement of the stars. And it's important to have the relevant knowledge and skills such as an education in astronomy. You'll also need a detailed plan so you can search a specific region of the sky, along with the determination to work hard and be ready for whatever life brings, such as a cloudy night or a finicky telescope. Any independent person or institution from any culture, researching the night sky with all these resources in place, would find the truthful existence of the amazing Orion Nebula.

Science plays a central role in uncovering objective universal truths because it uses reason, logic, and analysis to systematically explore and uncover factual events and objects. In its purest form, science pursues truth. Now, there are occasions when the pursuit of scientific truth breaks down, but those setbacks usually occur when other factors are at play. For instance, a scientist may lack objective clarity due to unhealthy psychological or spiritual beliefs. Or they may be overworked and fatigued. Perhaps their integrity has broken down due to a pining for fame or validation. When these occur, there are disruptions to safeguarding truth in the scientific process. Luckily, when these breakdowns occur, they can always be addressed, for the scientific method involves rigorous questioning, examining conclusions, and having independent verification through the investigations of others.

> Objective universal truths are factual, existing beyond the individual.

Humans are still very early in the process of exploring our world, so it goes without saying that we will sometimes get things wrong, even when there are protections in place, for we are not flawless. But if we cultivate the right attitude, the right resources, and the right approach, we are very likely to find objective universal truths.

It's important to note that not all truths are objective universal truths. For example, it may be a statement of fact that I had a dream about lions last night. While this experience may be a fact, it is not an objective universal truth because it cannot be independently verified by others. Also, objective universal truths are not necessarily the whole truth or the complete truth. We may discover an objective truth, but that does not mean that we have found the ultimate truth of the matter. This is something we will delve into later.

# Falsehoods

Falsehoods are the opposite of truth. They are not based on reality, and they are not objective facts. Falsehoods are often presented as truth, yet they lack objective, factual existence. In other words, they are not in alignment with reality. When falsehoods are presented as fact, it can lead to much confusion and chaos.

Falsehoods are borne out of ignorance, confusion, mistakes, distortions, misinformation, deception, lies, frauds, or delusions. At times, our falsehoods are unintentional; we may unknowingly present a falsehood when we are misinformed or make a mistake. Other times, falsehoods are intentional; they are deliberate actions made to deceive or defraud others. The spread of intentional falsehoods arises out of conscious motivations (wanting to sway a vote in one's favor) and unconscious motivations (a mother tells her child that "college is useless" when unconsciously, she fears being left alone). In any case, whether falsehoods are intentional or unintentional, they are still untrue and potentially damaging.

Sadly, in our current world, deception is commonplace. Many consider the peddling of falsehoods to be the norm these days – if you can get away with it. But for the rest of us, it's exhausting to constantly be on the lookout for them. The vigilance required to safeguard our sanity and our livelihood leaves us fatigued and exasperated.

Deception comes in many forms – lying, cheating, false advertising, altered pictures, distorted information, or leaving out important facts. With the advancement of technology, the spread of falsehoods is becoming pervasive and difficult to manage. With social media, it's hard to catch and control the explosion of falsehoods when algorithms are set up to prioritize themes that pull for the highest views. We all have seen occasions where deceptions have proliferated, causing widespread chaos, fear, and even hyper-consumerism as people attempt to stave off a perceived threat. Across the world, social media has been used to promote false allegations of election fraud, resulting in disruption and turmoil in many countries. Whenever misinformation spreads, it has the potential to undermine individuals, families, communities, and entire societies.

Deception also comes in mixtures of fact and falsehood. A good example of this mixture can be seen in the use of data, where facts are used to create an impression of truth, or the data is presented in a such a way that it distorts the truth. In both cases, the message being communicated is false. Imagine that you're trying to sell ten puppies, and two of them have peed on the floor. It would be a misrepresentation to say, "80% of our puppies never pee on the floor!" In this example, the deception is subtle, yet it is still a deception. Can you recall a time when information was presented to you in a distorted way that misrepresented the truth? How did you feel when you realized that the truth had been manipulated?

We can also experience *personal distortions* of truth – a form of self-deception. We can believe falsehoods about ourselves, others, and the world, deceiving ourselves about important issues. For example, we may distort the truth about our health, our aging, or our weight. We may deceive ourselves about our work life, thinking we can handle the job, when in fact, our job is compromising our health and wellbeing. Or we can deceive ourselves about what is going on in the world. We may tell ourselves "Everything's fine," or "Somebody else will fix it," when we witness devastation and chaos. Sadly, when we delude ourselves, we set the conditions for ongoing suffering in our lives.

> ### Telling Yourself the Truth
>
> When you have a moment to yourself, take some time to reflect on these questions. Be truthful and hold an attitude of gentleness and kindness toward yourself.
>
> *Is there something you believe about yourself that deep down you know isn't the truth?
>
> *Is there something you tell yourself that's not true to make yourself feel better... to make your life easier... or avoid conflict?
>
> *Is there something that your internal critic says about you that is just not the truth?
>
> As you reflect on these self-deceptions, how do they make you feel?
>
> This practice may initially bring up uncomfortable feelings, yet can you imagine how this awareness might lead to a more candid, honest, healthier life? As you become more comfortable telling yourself the truth, you will open doors that lead to a more successful and fulfilling life.

Falsehoods come in many flavors. As we cultivate our deep thinking, we awaken to all the variations falsehoods can take. With this discernment, we are empowered to see any untruths and address them for what they are — untruthful narratives that adversely impact us and the world. When we clearly recognize falsehoods and truth, we are destined to become more successful.

# Partial Truths

Can there be different truths about a given issue? I don't think so. I believe that there is only one truth, but we can each hold different *pieces* of the truth. This is what is referred to as "partial truths." The information we are holding is real and true, but it may not be the whole truth. Often, what we see as the truth is dependent upon our own perspective and orientation. The part we are looking at is indeed truthful (based on objective reality), but it's only one piece of the whole picture.

Problems can arise when we take our partial truth as the whole truth. In our confusion, we may not realize that we are in possession of only a piece of truth. If we are attached to our version of the experience, chaos and confusion can ensue when others present different views. A classic example of this dilemma is found in the parable of the three blind men and the elephant. In the old Indian parable, a wise king asks three blind men to describe an elephant. The first man feels the trunk and finds it to be long, thick, and wiggly. The man says, "Now I know about an elephant. He is exactly like a snake." The second man feels the leg and says, "What are you saying? Anybody can see that it is round and tall, like a tree." The third blind man feels the elephant's ear and says, "You don't know what you're talking about! The elephant is like a great fan!"

They each experienced a *piece* of the elephant – a partial truth – which they took as the whole truth. From our bigger perspective, we can see how they could be confused. From their narrow vantage point, the more inclusive truth – the whole elephant in *all* its majestic fullness – was lost to them.

In another example, years ago, my wife Maureen took our 3-year-old daughter and her friend Lyle on a drive through the countryside. Each child was in their car seat, positioned at opposite windows in the back seat of the car. As Maureen was driving by the fields, Lyle looked out his window and yelled, "Cows! I see cows!" My daughter looked out her window to an empty field and said, "There are no cows! I don't see cows!"

Adamantly, Lyle yelled, "There *are* cows! They're right *there!*" The two friends proceeded to argue about this for the next mile, each trying to convince the other that they were right! From a bigger perspective, we can see the whole truth in this account, as well as a little humor!

In a third example, in the late 17th century, Sir Isaac Newton proposed that light was a particle, while the Dutch physicist Christiaan Huygens believed that light was a wave. Then in 1801, British physicist, Thomas Young, did an experiment in which he demonstrated that light functions as a wave. Scientists believed the mystery was solved! But in 1905, Albert Einstein demonstrated that light consisted of particles, known as photons. It wasn't until 1927 that these two partial truths were brought together, when Clinton Davisson and Lester Germer proved that light functions both as a wave *and* a particle. This amazing fact – the duality of the wave/particle phenomenon – opened a new door to quantum mechanics. Through the ongoing reflection and experiments of many scientists, a bigger picture was revealed.

These three stories illustrate how different perspectives hold different pieces of a larger truth. Our viewpoints are always dependent on *what* we encounter and *how* we look at things. Something may appear to be the truth from one angle, yet not from another, just as my daughter and her friend experienced on their drive. These stories illustrate the importance of holding a bigger, "not knowing" outlook. When we keep our minds open to different viewpoints, we can amass much more information to find a larger understanding of what is truth.

It's important to remember that our perspective is colored by many variables – the instruments we use to look at something, the beliefs we carry into our investigation, and our orientation to the object: Are we seeing it from above, behind, or below? Are we close or far away? These conditions, as well as our mindstates, can impact our perceptions of what we see and experience.

While it may seem that different assessments are in conflict or competing with each other, from the broader perspective of a more inclusive truth, they are not in conflict. If we take a wider view, we can often see that things are in fact congruent. For example, if one were to fly a drone above the car that my daughter and her friend were in, they would see that on one side of the road there were cows in the field, and on the other side of the road, the field was empty –same scenario, different orientation.

There are no real competing truths, there is only one truth. But there *can* be competing ideas, beliefs, and interpretations based on our narrow experience. If we treat our partial truth as the whole truth and don't seek to understand the bigger picture, it can lead to conflict, harm, and mistrust of each other. In some versions of the elephant parable, the men argue and then come to blows over their opinions! This is one that way wars, oppression, and violence arise: When humans cling to their partial views of truth, it puts the world in chaos.

When we understand that we might be holding partial truths, it opens us up to more curiosity, a willingness to learn, and humility regarding our viewpoint. When we are open-minded, we can listen to others' knowledge and experience and include it in our investigations. Together, we can combine our truths to reveal a more complete, inclusive picture of the truth. In doing so, we will have a richer, more expansive perspective on the world. If the three blind men had been open to listening to each other, they could have developed a broader understanding of "elephant." When we incorporate others' perspectives, we are empowered to see the whole elephant; the whole countryside; that light functions as a wave *and* a particle, and our knowledge of the world and the universe will expand for the benefit of all.

This brings us to another question: When we put our partial truths together, do we *always* get the whole truth?

# The Whole Truth

People like to talk about the "whole truth" when it comes to certain issues. But do we ever have the whole truth? We may have the whole truth on whether or not it rained yesterday in our backyard, but when we encounter more complex issues, we often find that we don't have the *whole* truth or ultimate truth. In the larger issues of life, our understanding of truth is often in a state of discovery and evolution – it grows and evolves. But this does not necessarily invalidate or wipe out earlier truths. Oftentimes, broader truths *incorporate* earlier or partial truths into a more cohesive and comprehensive understanding of what is true.

In the last category, our discussion on light (as a wave and a particle) demonstrated our evolving understanding of truth. To further highlight this, let's consider another vignette from Sir Isaac Newton. While drinking tea one evening under the shade of an apple tree, Newton saw an apple fall to the ground and wondered, "*Why does the apple always descend perpendicularly to the ground?*"

Using his deep thinking, Newton formulated the law of gravity. Hundreds

> In the larger issues of life, our understanding of truth is often in a flux state of evolution, expanding and advancing over time.

of years later, some scientists remarked that Einstein's general theory of relativity wiped out Newton's theories on gravity. But I don't think this is a helpful way to think about it. It is more valuable to consider that Einstein *incorporated* or *expanded* on Newton's theories to create a broader understanding of gravity. In other words, there was an evolution of our understanding. It is likely that Einstein would never have reached his conclusions without Newton's theory. And besides, Newton's laws of gravitation are still used today to launch rockets into space.

Our understanding of the truth keeps evolving. As new knowledge emerges through the use of our computers and technology, Einstein's theories of gravity will likely be elaborated upon and evolve in the future. But the previous truths will not be erased; our understanding will simply broaden and deepen. Isaac Newton understood this idea. He discovered his three laws of motion by building on the work of earlier scientists such as Galileo, Copernicus, and René Descartes. As Newton famously said, "If I have seen further than others, it is by standing upon the shoulders of giants."

# Unknowns

When it comes to the truth, there is a lot that is unknown. There are the things that we recognize as unknown – like how many planets are in the universe – but there are many more unknown truths that we aren't even aware of. A hundred years ago, we only knew of the Milky Way galaxy, yet hundreds of billions of other galaxies were there all along. When it comes to existence and our human life, there are many unknown truths: *What is out there in the "Great Beyond?" How did life form? What happens to us after we die? What is the nature of consciousness?* The amount of what is unknown is unfathomable.

Just because we know a lot of details about something, doesn't necessarily mean that we understand it in its totality. Consider the brain. We know a vast amount about the brain, so we often believe that we understand how it works. We learned about it in school… There has been extensive research on it… We perform successful medical procedures on the brain… And we can describe thousands of details and facts about it. And yet, how the brain *really* works is still very much a mystery to us.

> ### Meeting the Unknown
>
> When you think about how many unknown truths there are, do you get excited about this idea, or does it bring up stress in you?
>
> As you ponder the many unknowns in the universe, what happens in your body? Do you feel tingly and excited... neutral... or perhaps a sense of contraction or anxiety?
>
> What stories do you tell yourself about the unknown?

Our relationship to the unknown greatly impacts our willingness to engage in exploration, or shy away from it. For some people, contemplating unknown truths and mysteries is exciting, stimulating, and thought-provoking. For others, it can be confusing or overwhelming, triggering anxiety as we struggle to accept that we don't know the truth of a situation. If we are uncomfortable with our idea of the "unknown," we might avoid or deny what we do not understand. In order to feel secure, we may hold tightly to what is familiar and known, unwilling to budge from the comfort of our position. Or we may pretend to know about things that are in fact unknown. This is evident when people make up stories to quell their uncertainty. This played out during the Covid-19 pandemic: Some people pushed various "cures" that turned out to be ineffective or harmful. If we are unable to tolerate the unknown, our explorations into the truth of matters will be thwarted, often to our detriment. To have a healthy foundation in truth, we need to release our fears of the unknown, so we can embrace our explorations fully.

# Metaphors

Another experience that relates to truth centers around metaphors. Metaphors are figures of speech that are symbolic of something else. To understand this category, it can be helpful to return to the teachings of our high school English class. *Literal truths* are facts based in reality, such as, "The sun is very hot!" *Metaphorical truths* use symbolic descriptions to describe or represent a true condition. For example, if you have a friend who is wild, big, and roaring every time he gets upset, it would be a metaphorical truth to say, "He's a bear when he is angry!" It's not true that he is a bear, but it is true that his actions are bear-like, which is the metaphor.

Another metaphor is the phrase, "To throw the baby out with the bathwater." One isn't going to really throw a baby out with the bathwater, but this example points to those moments when we want to eliminate something that is stressful, only to end up discarding something that is precious or valuable: In the heat of our frustration, we end a relationship, quit a job we love, or walk away from an opportunity because we cannot handle the tension. Only when we come back to our senses do we realize what we have lost.

Problems can arise when people take metaphorical statements to be literal truth. Imagine someone saying in a moment of frustration, "Argh!! I want to kill myself!" They don't really want to kill themselves, but if someone misunderstands this to mean the literal truth, it can lead to upsetting consequences. Other difficulties occur when an analogy or metaphor doesn't *fit* the actual truth of the situation. Imagine a doctor or political leader trying to have a thoughtful, caring discussion on how best we can approach the end of life with acceptance and grace, and a news reporter says, "He's a vulture, plotting your death!" In this case, the metaphor is a falsehood; it is being used to distort the truth, since this was not the doctor or politician's intention at all.

When we take the time to thoughtfully reflect on the intention being conveyed in metaphors, we can discern a deeper truth and avoid unwanted or harmful consequences. In our quest to find the truth, it behooves us to understand the use of metaphors so we can work with them in skillful ways.

# Fiction and Fantasy

When it comes to fiction and fantasy, this category is most definitely not the truth. But let's be clear – they are not meant to be the truth. Fictional scenarios are created through our imagination. They are something we "dream up" and we know that they are not true. Our imaginative scenarios may be inspired by the real world, and at times they may even appear realistic, but they do not express facts. Many times, they are completely improbable and unrealistic – you can search the world over, but you will not find a dragon. Like metaphors, our fictional imaginings may convey truthful experiences (they may portray important feelings, societal trends, and wisdom) but they are still fiction; they are not the truth.

Even though they are not the truth, creative fantasy and fiction can enrich our lives in countless ways. Movies, magic shows, fictional books, video games, and role plays – where we get to "pretend" that we are interacting with aliens, zombies, robots, wizards, and imaginary friends – are not only entertaining, but they can help us express ourselves more fully. They can also connect us to

> Fiction and fantasy are something we create through our imagination. They may be inspired by the real world and sound realistic, but they are not the truth.

our emotions and help us process challenges in our life. Great stories also connect and bond us to one another, encouraging us to engage with others in stimulating conversations – even with strangers. Think about the millions of people who have come together to read or watch *Harry Potter*, *The Lord of the Rings*, or the *Barbie* movie. Fantasy and fiction may not be the actual truth, but they often speak powerfully to truth when used skillfully.

Conversely, there are instances when fiction and fantasy can be harmful to us, even when we *cognitively understand* that they do not adhere to the real world. An example of this is found in horror films. We may know that they are make-believe, yet nonetheless, a scary story can wreak havoc on our mind, body, and heart, sometimes with devastating consequences. I have worked with countless children, young people, and adults who struggle with distressing anxiety brought on by exposure to intense horror media. While horror media is fictional, the fallout from this exposure is an unfortunate truth that can take months, and sometimes even years, to resolve.

In today's world, a wide range of destructive fiction is now propped up by AI, realistic-looking computer graphics, adrenaline-pumping scripts, sensual images, and sound effects meant to keep us "hooked" on fictional media. At times, these destructive forces are used to manipulatively shift our beliefs, our feelings, our emotions, and our social norms. We may be fed misleading racist propaganda, images or directives that threaten our self-esteem, or media that activates addictions such as gambling and pornography. When we succumb to the spellcraft of destructive fiction, it diminishes our quality of life. Fiction and fantasy may be entertaining and thought-provoking, but they are not the truth. We would do well to remember this and be mindful of their impact on our lives and the world.

# Ideas

Ideas, like fiction and fantasy, are products of our human imagination. However, there is a big difference between these two classifications. We know that fiction and fantasies are made up; we know that they are not the truth. But our ideas often involve truth, facts, and our interpretation of these things. Ideas are created as we ponder about the world, brainstorm, or daydream about various problems or scenarios in our lives: We contemplate an issue and speculate… Not knowing what the actual truth is, we dream up proposals or hypotheses about what is going on and what the truth might be. In other words, we make up ideas about the truth. Ideas and hypotheses are incredibly useful for they help us contextualize the world so we can work with it. Hopefully, our ideas reflect the truth.

Throughout history, humans have been making up ideas about the things they see and experience in the world. Today, we know for a fact that the earth orbits the sun – this is empirical knowledge. But there was a time when we did not know this: Humans would look to the night sky and watch the stars move across the sky, noticing that the stars gradually shifted

> Ideas are hypotheses and theories as to what we think the truth might be.

their position throughout the seasons of the year. This fact inspired them to come up with ideas and hypotheses about what exactly was happening. Many earlier humans attributed the movements of the stars to the whims of gods and goddesses. But over time, as we evolved and developed, new ideas began to emerge.

In the second century, the Greek Egyptian scholar and astronomer, Ptolemy, had a new idea – Earth was the center of the universe. In his theory, the Sun, stars, planets, and Moon all revolved around a stationary Earth.

Using complex mathematical calculations, he attempted to explain his elaborate ideas and interpretations, trying to prove that Earth was the center of the universe. While his thoughtful ideas were based on his observations, they were not the factual truth. However, Ptolemy presented them so compellingly, his ideas spread, and they were taken as the truth in the Islamic world and throughout Europe for the next 1400 years!

Many centuries later in the 16$^{th}$ century, Copernicus, a Polish astronomer, had another idea. He looked at the movements of the stars across the night sky and proposed that Earth was spinning on its axis and this rotation accounted for the "movement" of stars in the night sky. Not only that, but he also proposed that Earth was orbiting around the sun, along with all the other planets. In his hypothesis, Copernicus speculated that the sun – not Earth – was the center of our universe. And it would be another hundred years before Italian philosopher, astronomer, and mathematician, Galileo – armed with an improved telescope and detailed, factual observations – proved that Copernicus's idea was in fact the truth: *The earth orbits the sun.* Even to this day, scientists and astronomers continue to generate new ideas about the cosmos, advancing our explorations and understanding of the universe.

When we take on the study of an object or event, we may initially uncover partial truths that at first seem irreconcilable. But as I stated earlier, there are no competing truths or competing facts. There may be competing "ideas" about the facts or competing "interpretations" of the facts – just as Ptolemy and Copernicus differed in their interpretations of the movements of the stars – but the truth is ever present; we just need to discover it. In many ways, mapping our solar system is a lot like mapping the great elephant: When we begin, we have a lot of ideas and partial truths. But if we hold an open mind and understand that we are working with ideas and partial truths, this is not a problem. Different ideas and hypotheses can benefit us, and fresh ideas can widen our perspective. When seeking the truth, it's best to keep an open mind and heart, along with a willingness to test out our ideas; doing this will help us more readily discover objective universal truths.

Envisioning ideas is a wonderful, fun, human faculty. Our ideas can be inspiring and lead us to new understandings and deeper truths about our existence. But until we have proof that our ideas are in fact true, we need to hold them lightly. If we treat our untested ideas as the truth, we can create havoc in our world, at times causing great harm to ourselves, others, and our planet. Ideas are great when they are used skillfully and in service to humanity, so let us treat them as theories until they are proven otherwise.

# Concepts

Much of our experience in the world is organized into conceptual thinking. *Concepts* are abstract ideas that we use to capture, group, and organize objects and information into specific classes, so we can better understand the objects and ideas and work with them. Concepts help us organize and navigate our world: If someone asks us to bring a chair in from the other room, we don't come back with a dog. We can also use concepts to deepen our understanding of things. For example, we might conceptualize things into the *human* and *non-human* world. From there, we can make further classifications: Humans can be classified into concepts such as *adults* and *children*, then further divided into *seniors, middle-aged, young adults,* and *adolescents, middle schoolers, toddlers,* and *infants*. The non-human world can be classified into *plants, animals, insects, earth,* and *water*. And further conceptualizations can be made out of each of these categories. The creation of concepts or classes allows us to organize our knowledge and infer how things in each class will function or be used, giving us a workable "map" for how to interact with the world. For instance, when we understand the concept of a "child," we don't expect a five-year-old to act like an adult.

Concepts are crucial to our functioning because they serve as building blocks for our thinking. We use concepts to organize our thoughts, as well as convey meanings and information. Concepts are found throughout the world – in every discipline, area of study, profession, and as a means to describe almost everything in life. We use concepts to understand and talk about law... education... plumbing... setting a table... running a race... xeriscaping... or sculpting a clay pot. We have mathematical and scientific concepts, visual, emotional, and musical concepts, and concepts that describe characteristics such as *beauty, friendship, equality, freedom,* and *justice.* Language is a concept. And the idea of a "concept" is itself, a concept! Without concepts, it would be impossible to discuss ideas and complex structures.

> Concepts are abstract ideas that we use to capture, group, and organize things into specific classes so we can better understand them and work with them.

Concepts are also borne out of our socialization. Because of this, the same concept may be used differently by diverse disciplines, people, and cultures. Consider the concept of "walking." In the American Southwest, walking can be a very laid-back stroll, even ambling at times. But in New York City or Boston, Massachusetts, you'll encounter "New York walking" or "Boston walking," a hurried, purposeful strut or jog, moving decisively, as if you have to get somewhere *fast*. If you are walking in either of these big cities and don't pick up the pace, you'll definitely be left behind, or worse yet, run over!

We can see these different understandings of concepts when we look at the norms of various cultures. For example, the idea of *personal space* is very different in India than it is in the United States. The concept of *wealth*, or what makes for a *rich life*, is viewed differently by industrialized nations and low- or middle-income countries. And across the world, the concept of *family* takes on many forms.

Some concepts are based on truth, others are not. Examples of truthful concepts include: *molecules* are made up of atoms; a *triangle* has three sides; and *mammals* are warm-blooded. These concepts are based on facts. But concepts can also be based on metaphors, fiction, and fantasy, and even the unknown. Dragons are well-known throughout the world yet they don't exist. There are also concepts based on ideas, meanings, beliefs, and intuitions. For example, many people hold different concepts of God.

Concepts are incredibly useful, but they can bring great harm when we confuse them for the truth. An example of this occurred in the 19th century when the concept of "phrenology" was touted as the new definitive way to understand and predict human functioning. Phrenologists studied the placement and measurement of bumps on the skull, creating a detailed map designed to predict personality traits and mental abilities in humans.

Phrenology posited many concepts. Some corresponded to the truth: For example, the idea that brain functioning influences our behavior. However, many of their concepts were based on falsehoods. Phrenologists claimed that brain functioning impacts the shape of the skull, so the contour of the skull could accurately predict personality traits. Armed with these concepts, phrenologists asserted that they could accurately diagnose pathology and unhealthy traits in people.

The public's embracing of phrenology resulted in many misdiagnoses and mistreatments. Phrenology maps were used to determine how to educate children, how to decide if someone was qualified for a job, or whom they should marry. It was even used to promote sexism and racism – phrenologists claimed that skull shape proved the inferiority of women and non-white races. The false concepts promulgated by phrenologists were very harmful.

Concepts and their organizing principles offer a great boon to humanity. They help us crystallize large amounts of information, discuss ideas and information, and work with big ideas in support of our evolution and growth. They work best when we bring clear awareness to our concepts – knowing which ones are based on truth, or falsehood. When we are clear about our concepts, they become important tools in support of our success.

# Beliefs and Meanings

The beliefs we carry, and the meanings displayed in our beliefs, greatly influence our experience of truth. A *belief* is a state of mind where we place our trust or confidence in a set idea. Our beliefs are built out of the *meanings* we've made of the world. As we go through life seeing, hearing, tasting, touching, and contemplating the world, we make associations to our experiences: touching a hot stove is *dangerous*; birdsongs are *soothing*; when my father yells, he is *angry*. We make meanings about our experiences, and in time, these meanings solidify into beliefs and stories about ourselves and the world, shaping our day-to-day experience. As an example, if someone refuses to speak to us after we share our opinion, we may think it means that *they are mad at us*, and over time we may come to believe that it is not okay to use our voice.

Like ideas and concepts, meanings and beliefs are distinct from objective facts. We can certainly *believe* something to be the truth, but unless it's been clarified or confirmed as an objective fact, we cannot rely on it as the truth. So, until it is proven to be true, it's important to treat our opinions as beliefs – to hold them with a lighter grasp, not giving them the weight we entrust to known truths. With this awareness, we can hold our beliefs as personal viewpoints or personal philosophies without positing that our beliefs are solid, known truths.

It's easy to see the importance of this when we reflect upon others' beliefs. As an experiment, consider a group of people whose beliefs are different from yours. Perhaps they hold different religious beliefs or different views on how women should be treated in the world. Do you consider their beliefs to be the *truth*? If not, would you want their beliefs to dominate your life or the world stage? When we reflect on others' beliefs, it's easy to see how personal viewpoints can wreak havoc when they are treated as objective truth. The same holds true when you flip the scenario: Imagine asking someone from another culture to allow *your* beliefs to rule the world. They may well cringe, fearing the implications of imposing your personal viewpoint on their world.

Beliefs are not the same as truths. Until a belief is demonstrated to be true, it is best to regard them as opinions, not objective truths. This does not mean that we cannot honor our own or another's beliefs. We can certainly respect the varied, wonderful beliefs that drive our and others' lives and hearts. But when it comes to a discussion of *truth*, we want to remain focused on objective, factual data.

Beliefs are important, for they mark what is significant and meaningful in our lives, adding tremendous richness to our human experience. They influence what work we go into, where we live, who we love, and whether we take risks and pursue our dreams. They also color our expressions of love, compassion, and service to others.

> Beliefs are distinct from the truth. A belief may turn out to be the truth, but until we confirm it as an objective fact, we regard it as a belief.

Our beliefs also play a role in how we use our technological advancements for they guide our moral and ethical choices. Should we use our technology to travel to other planets? Do we believe that Artificial Intelligence will help or destroy the world? What role should AI play in human evolution? Is it ethically right to launch technologies that we don't fully understand? Is it okay for a small group of people to make decisions that impact the whole world? Our beliefs will inform how we move forward with these powerful technologies.

In many respects, our beliefs give meaning to our human journey. If we believe that we are here for a purpose, we will consciously seek out a purposeful life. If we believe that life has no meaning, that will impact how we live. If we believe there is karma or accountability for our actions, we will strive to live righteously. If we believe that there is no karma or accountability – that we are just lifeforms evolving – that will influence how we live. If we happen to believe that *we are all God's children*, or *everyone and everything is a manifestation of One Consciousness*, it will affect how we treat human beings and the non-human world. As you can see, beliefs are integral to our overall functioning and wellbeing.

We carry many kinds of beliefs – cognitive, psychological, and spiritual – and they all shape our human existence. Ptolemy's cognitive belief that the sun revolved around Earth drove his scientific work. The psychological beliefs we carry about ourselves, others, and the world such as "The world is a safe place…" or "The world is a dangerous place…" directly influence our thoughts and behaviors. And our spiritual beliefs – our convictions about *that which is greater than ourselves*, and the mystery of the Universe – directly impact how we behave and conduct our lives. And the same is true for everyone else.

Beliefs are an integral part of our makeup as human beings. However, if we treat our beliefs as the truth, that is where things can break down. Equating beliefs with the truth is one of the biggest areas of confusion for humans and it is the cause of much suffering. As I stated earlier, there are no competing truths, but there can certainly be competing beliefs. And when people begin asserting competing beliefs, things can become vindictive as people get agitated and activated.

This happened in the late 1500s when an Italian philosopher, Giordano Bruno, proposed a larger, more integrative belief that went far beyond the work of Copernicus. Combining insights from his cognitive, psychological, and spiritual beliefs, he imagined a universe where the stars were distant suns surrounded by their own planets, some of which might even have life. He proposed an infinite universe, one without a center.

When Bruno presented his belief of an infinite universe without a center as a *fact*, he came into direct and intense conflict with the beliefs of the Catholic Church. The Church maintained that their belief – that God placed Earth in the center of the universe – was the *truth*. Due to the collision of these beliefs, Bruno was tried for heresy by the Roman Inquisition.

He was confined to prison for seven years and then burned at the stake in 1600.

Soon after, another astronomer, Galileo, was brought before the Inquisition because his scientific discoveries and beliefs contradicted the Church's assertion that the sun orbited the Earth. While he was not burned at the stake, he was condemned to life imprisonment, living out the rest of his life under house arrest.

Remarkably, Bruno's belief about stars being other suns did turn out to be the truth. However, to this date, we have yet to confirm that there is life on other planets.

Today, we are seeing a lot of confusion, chaos, and harm in our world arising out of the clash of beliefs – just as happened between Bruno and the Church. There are huge movements to "cancel out" scientific information that goes against beliefs that are being circulated in our media. This is why it is so important to understand the difference between *truth* and *beliefs*. Clarity about this issue allows us to build our world on a foundation of sound knowledge, while still recognizing and respecting others' beliefs.

> When we understand the difference between truth and beliefs, we can build our world on a solid foundation of clarity and wisdom, bringing the world into balance.

When we understand and accept that our own beliefs *may* or *may not* be the truth, it gives us a certain humility. It inclines us to be more open-minded and listen to others. It invites us to test our theories to see if they are, in fact, the truth. Holding our beliefs lightly also opens more curiosity when considering other people's perspectives, giving us greater capacity to learn, grow, and evolve. And finally, when we hold that our beliefs may not be the truth, it leads to less conflict. We are less likely to fight vehemently for our viewpoint when we know that our way of seeing things may not be *the truth*. When we hold a more comprehensive perspective on our beliefs, we invite greater understanding of the world and more successful social interactions.

# Intuitions

Intuition is an unconscious process where we realize an insight about something, usually in a flash, without the need for conscious reasoning or thinking. Often referred to as "gut feelings," intuitive insights can arise in connection with physical, emotional, cognitive, psychological, spiritual, or social consciousness, and they are more fully manifested when there is an integration of several of these areas. With our intuitive "hits," we often experience a sense of certainty, so our insights can significantly impact our behavior, our decision-making, and our creative endeavors. In this way, intuition can be instrumental in guiding our lives.

But like many other experiences (beliefs, ideas, concepts, etc.) intuitions – no matter how powerful and profound they are – are not the same as objective truths. The experience of having an intuition is a truthful event, but that does not mean that the *content* of the intuition is objectively real. Sometimes, intuitions are wrong. They may pick up on a partial truth, such as *someone is untrustworthy*, but our "hit" may not be based in reality: *He looks like a thief. I bet he robbed a store!* While our intuition may not always be based in fact, it can still give us valuable information. Personally, my intuitions have guided me throughout my life, even though I know they aren't definitive facts.

Intuitive thinking is an integral part of our human nature. It is developed through our experiences and learning, and as such, it is dependent on our conditioning. When we experience normal, healthy living, our intuitions are more likely to be sound and accurate. However, if we experience unhealthy or traumatic conditions, it may be hard for us to get reasonable insights. For instance, if you've been in a car accident, you may have an intuitive "hit" that driving is unsafe, or you're sure that an accident is going to happen every time you get in a car. But this kind of "intuition" is a form of traumatic anxiety left over from the accident; it is not your deep intuitive wisdom. Our intuitions can be instrumental in helping us live safe, healthy lives, but it is important to keep a clear perspective on the difference between intuition, traumatic responses, and objective truth.

> Although intuitions can be incredibly helpful and can be a powerful force in our lives, they are not the same as objective truth.

# Social Constructs

Social constructs are ideas that are created, developed, and accepted by a specific group of people as a way to organize their lives, understand themselves and others, and function more effectively in the world. They are products of human imagination, effort, and collaboration – agreed-upon realities that exist because people agree that they exist. As collectively created entities, social constructs are not objective universal truths.

Take for example, the idea of "nations." Nations are a social construct. Over time, humans have come to agree that people living within the boundaries of certain geographical areas, with a certain common history, speaking specific languages, and having certain shared beliefs, are considered to be *nations*. But nations aren't objective universal truths.

Humans made up this idea, the same way we have made up *money, forms of government, economic systems, laws, religion, race, calendars, cryptocurrency, and NFTs*. These are all examples of social constructs created by humans. We agree that they exist, even when this agreement is unconscious.

While the existence of social constructs is real (just as the existence of ideas, beliefs, and intuitions are real), a social construct may or may not correspond to anything in the real world. Consider the construct of "calendars." While we experience the unfolding of day and night, the social construct of a calendar organizes our "days" into seven-day "weeks" and twelve-month "years." Even when social constructs draw on facts such as daylight, dark, or seasonal changes, the construct itself is still not objective reality – it is an imagined, created structure.

Social constructs have likely existed since the beginning of human culture. It is unlikely that societies and cultures could have evolved without them. They have enabled large groups of people to come together to communicate about shared purposes and common goals and social constructs such as *armies, governments,* and *schools* have advanced the ambitions of humanity across the world for centuries.

> Social constructs are imagined, agreed-upon ideas used to organize societies.

An extremely important point to understand is that once social constructs are formed, humans tend to project a lot onto those constructs. We may project our psychological, spiritual, or cognitive beliefs onto the construct, as well as our ideas, intuitions, and values. Falsehoods can also be woven into social constructs. For example, *race* is a social construct, but when beliefs about the inferiority of people with different skin colors are put upon race, that makes for *racism*.

The vivid impact of our projections can be seen when you reflect on social constructs such as *democracy, education, capitalism, healthcare,* and *socialism*. Our beliefs about these institutions clearly impact our experience of them. People can be seen fighting for their impassioned versions of these institutions, believing that their conceptualization of the construct is the *right* version. Therefore, when working with social constructs, it behooves us to be mindful not only of the construct, but also the beliefs and values that are being projected onto the construct. Only when we understand the beliefs behind social constructs can we work with them effectively.

Since social constructs are created by humans and laden with our projections and beliefs, different people can look at the same social construct differently. Marriage offers a good example of this. While marriage is a common social construct, it is not an objective universal truth. Marriage did not always exist – it was created by humans and divergent groups and societies bring different ideas and beliefs to the concept of marriage. Some believe that marriage should be arranged by a wise adult, while others believe that it is a mutual choice by each partner. In certain groups and cultures, it is believed that one partner should be dominant in the marriage, while other cultures believe that there should be equality between the partners. And in some circles, marriage is seen as a contractual arrangement, while others view it as a religious observance. Societies and cultures also dictate who should get married, when one should get married, and how the marriage should be conducted.

There is nothing inherently wrong with having differing beliefs about marriage. Problems arise when we think our beliefs about marriage are the objective truth, not simply *beliefs*. No matter how vehemently we hold that our beliefs are the truth, our conviction does not make them the truth. As we grow into a more globalized society, we will encounter different social constructs that display divergent values and beliefs – beliefs that have served other cultures and countries for centuries. When we understand the important difference between beliefs and truths, it can open us up to fruitful discussions and expand our understanding of the role of social constructs. With this clarity, we can promote greater growth and harmony to create a more connected, equitable world.

Our social constructs have done much to help us advance our world. Throughout the history of humanity, they have helped us live together peacefully, build governments, establish educational systems, and organize people to work together. In other words, they have helped us develop the civic fabric of our communities. When our social constructs are created in healthy, thoughtful ways, they help us organize humanity and create sophisticated complex systems that advance our dreams and ambitions.

However, not all social constructs are healthy. Some are laden with harmful projections, falsehoods, and misinformation, making them very harmful. Throughout history, social constructs have been used by unhealthy people to promote self-serving agendas. They have been used to justify oppressive class systems. They have been implemented to persecute minority groups. And they have constructed to subjugate and enslave people, and even carry out genocides. They have also been used to mobilize hundreds of millions of people to carry out horrific wars. When our constructs are built upon falsehoods – especially manipulative fabrications – they lead to polarization, divisiveness, and conflict.

Since social constructs are a product of human imagination, they reflect our beliefs and ideas. As we have changed and evolved over millennia, our social constructs have also changed and evolved. When humans agree that a construct is no longer valid or necessary, we can let them go, and replace them with something more aligned with our new ideas and beliefs. Sometimes, the change comes quickly. Over the last centuries, we have witnessed a great restructuring in our understanding of gender, race, government, aging, sexuality, sports, and a whole host of social constructs. Today, women partake in many jobs once believed to be possible only for men. Older citizens are redefining what "old age" looks like. And many countries are recognizing the importance of honoring same sex marriages, embracing the social construct, "Love is Love." Facts do not change, but social constructs do. Whenever we expand our understanding of ourselves and the world, our psychological beliefs change, offering a new opportunity to evolve our social structures in fresh, progressive ways.

Social constructs carry immense power for our betterment or detriment, so it's important to see them for what they are. When we are clear that they are imagined ideas as opposed to objective reality, we are better equipped to evaluate their impact and usefulness. We can mindfully reflect on what is working or not working with them. We can assess whether they are advancing humanity and our well-being or creating harm and chaos for us. And importantly, we can consciously and deliberately upgrade our social constructs to reflect truth. In fact, the idea of committing to a collective vision of truth is a new social construct! If we commit to pursuing and advocating for truth on this planet, we can open doors to new possibilities, bring healing and peace to many divisions that exist in our world as we work to advance humanity's development. When we become conscious of social constructs and deliberately work to create healthy, balanced social norms, we will benefit not only in our own communities, but the world as a whole, for I believe, *we are all in this together.*

> **Our Malleable Social Constructs**
>
> I invite you to choose a specific social construct that interests you. It could be about a specific group of people or a social topic. Briefly define or describe the construct as you see it. Now, take a moment to reflect...
>
> *What is its purpose?
>
> *What beliefs and ideas do you project onto this construct?
>
> *What are some beliefs and ideas that other people project onto it?
>
> *Who is impacted by this construct?
>
> *Who benefits from it, and in what ways?
>
> *Is anyone harmed by it? In what ways?
>
> *How is the broader world impacted by this construct?
>
> *Would you like to change this construct? If so, in what ways would you change it?

# Mixtures and Combinations

In today's world, we often don't get the full truth. Frequently, information comes to us in a mixture of truths, falsehoods, fiction, beliefs, misunderstandings, or misinformation. Given this, it is up to us to sort through the information and tease out what is truth, what is a metaphor, what is fictional fantasy, what is untrue, and what is deliberate manipulation.

Many times, mixtures and combinations of truth and fiction are creatively assembled, creating compelling stories, novels, and movies that are entertaining and thought-provoking. Dragons mixed into medieval stories can inspire our sense of adventure. In a historical novel, a town may come alive through a mixture of truthful information and creative embellishments. We can be transported in time and space by computer-generated scenes crafted for an action-adventure movie or a space odyssey. In these instances, the negative impact of creative falsehoods can be quite benign. When truth and falsehoods are mixed for entertainment or to bring alive a teaching point, they can be of great service to our living and learning.

We encounter mixtures and combinations in all kinds of daily interactions. Your grandfather may weave fact and fiction together in his "tall tales." You might embellish a story with some not-so-true claims. And your neighbor may tell you that it's raining today (a true fact, as you stand with him, getting soaked in the rain) because "God is mad at everybody" (his belief). In these moments, mixtures and combinations seem harmless, but there are plenty of instances where they can be harmful, leading to much pain and chaos, particularly when the falsehoods are added in with the intent to confuse, mislead, or manipulate others.

> Frequently, information comes to us in a combination of truths, falsehoods, fiction, beliefs, misunderstandings, or misinformation.

These days, we are seeing maladaptive combinations increasingly used in social media, newscasts, advertising, and political messaging, all with the intention of influencing the viewpoints and behavior of the populace. Advertisers often mix truth and falsehoods to influence our buying trends: They may claim that their soft drink "energizes" you and produces "significant weight loss," when it is simply loaded with caffeine. In news organizations, it is not uncommon to overfocus on volatile stories to increase viewership – making it look as if a city is "loaded" with crime, when in fact the crime numbers are decreasing. And some politicians lie in order to get our vote: "Your wages don't buy much! And it's my opponent's fault!" When falsehoods are mixed with truths in toxic combinations, it can lead to tremendous divisiveness, sometimes to the point of flaring panic, riots, wars, or the collapse of communities.

For our health and wellbeing, it's important to recognize that most of our information comes in some form of mixtures and combinations. There may well be truth in the offering, but if we look closely, we are likely to find beliefs, falsehoods, fabrications, and sometimes, manipulations mixed in. Understanding this reality helps us be judicious when we assess information. Later in this book, we will look at specific ways to sort through distortions of truth.

# Personal Truth

No discussion on truth is complete without addressing the classification of *personal truth*. We frequently use the term "personal truth" to indicate a strongly held belief or intuition as in, "Well, that might be your truth, but it's not *my* truth." I believe that using the word truth in this context can be confusing and even harmful for it doesn't point to actual truth, so much as to one's convictions, and we know what can happen when people push their convictions!

Given this, I propose that anytime we use the word *truth* – be it personal, collective, mine, or yours – we ensure that we are referring to that which is objective and factual. If we say, "My truth is..." it should be followed up by facts and based on reality, not our beliefs or imaginings. "Given that I've seen pictures of Earth from space, I know that the earth is round." In this way, we stand on solid ground.

If we are not discussing a factual reality or we don't know for sure if something is objectively true, it's best to say, "Well, I believe that..." putting forth our beliefs, ideas, intuitions, and imaginings as personal viewpoints that we adhere to. "Well, you might think that. But I believe women should have the right to vote." Using these types of proclamations can soften the "sting" when we disagree with someone, for we are not fighting about TRUTH, we are speaking to our convictions.

One reason why we treat our beliefs as the truth and fight so vehemently for them is that in our society, beliefs are often treated as less important or less vital than facts. But this is not the case. Our beliefs are vital and important – strongly held personal beliefs and intuitions provide important direction and guidance in our lives. They speak to inner convictions and values that are dear to our hearts and counsel our behavior.

When someone dismisses our beliefs, it can feel as though they are dismissing us or our values – an experience that can trigger anger and fear. If we can remember that people's beliefs express important values to them, we can honor their beliefs and values while maintaining a clear understanding that beliefs are not necessarily objective facts.

Much of the pain and confusion we see in our world stems from people treating their personal beliefs and intuitions as facts. It may be true that we have powerful personal experiences. Having these experiences is a fact. It can also be true that we create meanings about our experiences – we form ideas and beliefs about what happened and what it signifies – but these are *ideas* and *beliefs*, informed by our conditioning and personal perspective. If we treat our ideas and beliefs as factual truth, we can miss the actual truth of the matter and make decisions that lead us away from a truly successful life.

Imagine for a moment that you've had a powerful dream, and in this dream, you left your partner and kids. Having the dream was a fact; it is also a fact that the dream consisted of images of you leaving your family. But if you interpret the dream as evidence that you should leave your partner and kids, this concrete interpretation could be devastating. It would not be helpful to say to your partner, "Having this dream, I know that I'm meant to leave you." Instead, it would be wiser to view the advice in the dream figuratively, rather than literally. Exploring it, you might decide that your dream is actually an unconscious nudging, pushing you to attend to a long-term difficulty in your relationship. Leaving your family may not be what is needed at all; perhaps all that is needed is some couple's therapy.

Given that our interpretation of events may not always be factual, it is important that we don't treat them as truth. Instead, it is best to separate out the objective truth (we had an experience) from our interpretation *about* that experience. While it may be true that we had a dream, an intuition, or a premonition, we may not know what it actually means.

One final point regarding personal truth concerns *memory*. People often believe that their memories recall the truth of a matter. But memories don't always reflect facts. Having a memory is a fact, but the content of the memory may not always be factual. Many studies have shown that memories can be influenced, shaped, changed, or distorted by many factors. For example, when tragedies or accidents occur, it is not uncommon for different witnesses to report unsimilar scenarios for the same event. In another example, a good friend of mine has kept a journal for over 45 years, and he recently began reading through his older entries. Delving into his accounts of his life has revealed an interesting paradox: The details in his journal regarding certain events are very different from how he remembers them now. Jokingly, he told me, "I think my journal got it wrong!" The fact that our memories can change doesn't negate our memories. It is just something to be aware of and consider as we contemplate truth.

> Although strongly held personal beliefs and intuitions provide guidance and direction in our lives, this does not mean they are objective truths.

## Summary

Reflecting on these fifteen categories of experience (objective truth, ideas, beliefs, social constructs, etc.) and their relation to truth gives us a broader perspective and understanding of truth. In everyday experience – watching the news, talking with friends, flipping through social media – we get glimpses of ideas, beliefs, truths, falsehoods, and mixtures of these combinations as people relate their experiences, viewpoints, and agendas. With intention and practice, we can become deep thinkers and consciously discern these different types of experiences and the impact they are having on our lives and the world. When we grasp the difference between objective truths, beliefs, ideas, and intuitions, it's a game changer. It gives us solid ground to stand on as we navigate real-world experiences and encounter the interpretations that we and others bring to our life experiences. When we recognize the difference between objective, factual truth and these other types of experience, we are greatly empowered to uphold the truth.

With this framework, we can navigate the world in skillful and successful ways. Embracing the truth, we become informed, emboldened, and inspired to live authentically, speak to truth, and express our True Nature. Over two thousand years ago, the Buddha reportedly said, "Three things cannot be long hidden: the sun, the moon, and the truth." In the end, truth will win. If we align ourselves with the truth, we are ready to create an empowered, truthful, just world.

# Section Three

# Working With Truth

# Working With Truth

If we wish to advance our pursuit of truth, it is important to do some personal reflection on our relationship with truth. It's also important that we develop new skills so we can effectively advocate for truth. When we understand our own strengths and weaknesses in this area, we can release the fears, blocks, or biases that might be hindering our capacity to perceive and support the unfolding of truth. For example, if you were raised to be suspicious of others, it may be hard for you to accept the truth even when it is presented with objective facts. When we release our limiting or unhealthy conditioning, we empower ourselves to become advocates for truth.

In the following sections, I offer reflections and tools that can strengthen your capacity to seek out truth and skillfully discuss its implications with others. We begin with an exploration of the role that truth plays in your life.

# Our Relationship With the Truth

When working with the truth, it's important to reflect on our own relationship to it. Personally, I believe that humans have an innate drive to prioritize the truth. Yet this drive is shaped by many factors such as life experiences and our conditioning. If our conditioning was full of healthy, balanced instruction and plenty of safety, chances are good that we can discern between truth and fabrication. But if we grew up in a harsh or unhealthy environment, or lacked sufficient instruction, we may be confused about truth. In an unhealthy environment, others' beliefs may have been sold to us as truths; we may have been deceived about the truth; or we may have endured many painful experiences that hinder our ability to recognize truth when it's presented to us. In a similar way, we may not trust the truth, or we may form beliefs and stories about ourselves and the world that we *think* are the truth, but they are in fact, not truth. Additionally, if we engage in high uses of unhealthy media (which perpetuates so many falsehoods) we may drift further away from a truthful reality.

As you begin to seek out and work with truth in your life, I invite you to reflect on your personal beliefs concerning truth. Doing so will give you a clear sense of your foundation with truth and highlight areas that you may need to address or heal as you seek to become an advocate of truth.

> ### Your Relationship with Truth
>
> By now, you've encountered many new ideas about truth and the ways that distortions of truth can harm humanity and our planet. At this moment, how important is truth to you?
>
> *Do you believe that truth is critical to our well-being? If so, how are you inspired to advocate for truth?
>
> *What might keep you from advocating for truth in our world? Perhaps you feel some fear, or you believe that you're not ready to stand up for truth – you don't fully grasp the concepts presented here, or you don't know how to engage others skillfully.
>
> *If you are passionate about advocating for truth, where can you find support for yourself? Perhaps you'd like to invite some friends or colleagues to this venture. Maybe you would like to do some further study on advocacy. When we develop our skills and collaborate with allies, we are empowered to change ourselves and the world.

Whatever your relationship with truth, *it has been built on your past experiences*. If we grew up with safe, honest interactions, we will have a good sense of truth. If we have been manipulated or duped in the past, we may have a very tenuous relationship with the truth. Getting clear about what truth is and isn't, gives us a new opportunity to align ourselves with truth and make decisions that are based on reality, not the agendas of others, or misinformation. When we know what truth is we are empowered to create a very successful life.

Truth has always been clear, real, honest, and *true*. It stands the test of time, regardless of what people believe or don't believe at any given moment. People may believe that the world is round or flat, but their beliefs do not impact the actual shape of the planet. Truth is reliable and dependable, so we can rest our hearts upon it. As the saying goes, "The truth will set you free."

# How Truth is Determined

When working with truth, we often bring lots of ideas, beliefs, and intuitions to our explorations, but how do we know when we are seeing the truth? The core determination of truth is *rational evidence* – do we have objective facts that confirm, corroborate, validate, or prove the matter? If so, then we can rest assured that we are dealing with the truth. But when it comes to evidence, we also need to make sure that it is reliable. If our evidence has been compromised, such as when a pharmaceutical team skews its data to create monetary profits, it becomes useless to us. When we have good evidence, we are on solid ground.

Many times, we get our evidence from direct experience: If we are standing in the rain, we know that it is truly raining. But we need to be clear that our experience and our *interpretation* of our experience are two different things. Our interpretation may not be true at all, so to stay on solid ground, it's best to stay with the facts.

While it's helpful to have direct evidence for determining the truth of a matter, we can't personally validate everything. At these times, it is best to engage other sources to find rational evidence to determine the truth of a matter. We can utilize articles and books, online sources, governmental and institutional reports, news organizations, historical records, and speak with others who are familiar with the topic. For instance, if you want to clarify some family history, your grandmother may be the best source. It can also be helpful to turn to experts and people who are authorities on a topic. This includes masters, professionals, scholars, and specialists in their fields of expertise. Oftentimes, these professionals are part of organizations and institutions that can also be trusted to give truthful evidence.

When it comes to "experts," we also want to make sure that our source is conversant with the topic at hand. For instance, if we want to assess that our brakes are functioning correctly, it is best to go to a car mechanic; we don't ask a baker to assess our brakes. It's also important to make sure that our source is credible and reliable. Since truth is based on rational evidence, the designation of "expert" has to be based on evidence. Our expert needs to have the right training… to have practiced their trade for enough time to be competent… they must thoroughly investigate and study the topic at hand… they need to be clear about what they know and don't know… and their information should be accurate and impeccable; based on evidence through their practice and work. And if they get things wrong, they need to be willing to acknowledge their mistakes, retract the misinformation, and work hard to curtail those kinds of missteps in the future.

Sometimes, we need to dig deep to determine the credibility of a source. We may need to investigate their qualifications or fact-check their claims. For example, we might ask: Are they transparent about where their evidence comes from? Do they cross-check their information? How do their biases impact their work? Do they have an agenda? If we are engaging with a news organization, we might ask who finances them or what their political leanings are, taking time to reflect on how this might influence their reporting. Scrutinizing the sources of our information gives us a good sense of whether we can trust the information, or not. Luckily, there are many institutions that analyze and catalog the integrity and political orientations of businesses, organizations, and information sites to help us locate reliable sources. When our experts are informed, credible, and have good ethics, we are empowered through their wisdom.

One last point on sources. When looking for truth, it can be incredibly helpful to engage different sources of information. Like the three blind men, we will comprehend much more of the elephant if we take in perspectives that lie outside our conditioning. When we gather information from a wide variety of sources – contemplating other cultural and religious beliefs, as well as political leanings and viewpoints – we can encounter information that opens our mind, broadens our perspective, and deepens our wisdom. If we live in the United States, we may be greatly illuminated by reviewing news sources from other countries. If we consider ourselves "liberal," we might seek out reputable "conservative" sources, and vice versa. When we open ourselves to divergent viewpoints, we see a bigger picture, giving us a knowledgeable, informed perspective. Too often, people seek out information only from the sources that align with their personal beliefs and biases. While this may be comforting, it locks us in an "information bubble" that can lead to ignorance and close-mindedness. Humanity does much better when we listen to divergent perspectives to become more fully informed. Taking in another's wisdom expands our mind and our capacity for critical thinking.

# Cognitive Skills That Support Our Investigation

When it comes to determining the truth, it helps to have sharp cognitive capacities that can help us discern and organize what is before us in our investigations. Following are some important faculties that help us get the job done.

**Purposeful Skepticism**

When we hear the word *skepticism*, it can conjure up a variety of meanings: being close-minded, not believing, or guarding against gullibility. But if we look at the origins of this word, we find a more positive definition. Skepticism derives from the Greek word "skepsis," meaning *examination, inquiry, and consideration*. In other words, skepticism entails being focused and clear-headed when we encounter questionable information. When we employ *purposeful skepticism*, we bring a conscious, balanced questioning to our examination, with the clear intention of uncovering the truth. While some use skepticism as a defensive tactic (questioning or pushing away everything that is uncomfortable for them), the pragmatic use of purposeful skepticism is to investigate the truth while resisting the urge to make determinations before we have the necessary facts: We carefully track the details... systemize our knowledge... then use the information to grow and evolve as humans. In today's world, we are seeing a massive breakdown in critical thinking. People are peddling information without pausing to reflect on whether the information is true. Purposeful skepticism can help us cut through deception and distortions to reveal the truth in these matters, helping us live more successfully.

One area where purposeful skepticism is abundantly used is in the realm of science. For centuries, scientists and researchers have extolled the role of purposeful skepticism – so much so, they have incorporated it into the *scientific method*. The scientific method is a process used to objectively establish the verification of facts through testing and experimentation. It involves many steps to accurately quantify truth and facts: One begins with making an observation, then forms a hypothesis about the observation. Armed with their hypothesis, they can then posit a prediction, then conduct experiments to see if their hypothesis bears out. They analyze the results (the evidence), employing purposeful skepticism with the intention of keeping the observations clean and clear of personal biases.

> Purposeful skepticism is conscious, balanced questioning with a clear purpose. It is a skill used to investigate and verify the truth.

Scientists know that personal beliefs and biases, mistakes in the lab, and misinformation can compromise the integrity of research and analysis. For this reason, they revere purposeful skepticism and invite other scientists to bring their purposeful skepticism to cross-examine their work. Across the world, experiments are replicated, analyzed, and scrutinized many times over in the service of documenting the truths of the universe. Their attention to certainty and stoicism has developed a reliable and credible path for the discovery of truth, leading to phenomenal advances in science and technology.

We, too, can use purposeful skepticism in our day-to-day lives. When we bring thoughtful contemplation to what is before us, we are more likely to extract the truth when scrolling through social media, listening to the news, attending a political rally, or listening to others. We can also use purposeful skepticism to awaken more wisdom regarding our own biases, psychological ideologies, cultural conditioning, and spiritual beliefs. For instance, we can question the inner psychological beliefs and stories we tell ourselves. Is it actually true that I'm *stupid... lazy... can't handle the stress?* Is it true that *I'm the smartest person in the room?* We might also bring some purposeful skepticism to the stories we have heard about others and their cultures – stories that may incite racism, desires for privilege over others, or seeing other people as "not us." *Is it true that homeless people are just lazy deadbeats?* How did these beliefs get embedded into our minds and culture? Purposeful skepticism gives us the tools to dig down into our own conditioning and explore why we believe what we believe.

As humans, it's important to examine our beliefs and biases for our presumptions often interfere with our ability to see the truth clearly. As an example, consider the long-held belief that "women are weak." This belief blocked our collective capacity to see women as viable contributors in science, governing, the military, and business for *centuries*. And while it was known for centuries that Earth orbits the sun, the Catholic Church did not acknowledge this fact until the 19th century, creating a noxious condition that hampered scientific exploration in Western countries. Whenever we take our conditioning and beliefs at face value, we are at risk of being uninformed, duped by others, or worse, set up to unwittingly spread misinformation that works against humanity's best interests. Purposeful skepticism empowers us to question information, keeping an open mind and the sensitivity needed to discern truth from non-truth. Anytime we are investigating a topic, contemplating a matter that is important in our lives, or watching the news and we sense that something is "off" for us, it is wise to question what we are looking at and bring in some purposeful skepticism to clarify our understanding of the situation. Below is an exercise that can help you make use of purposeful skepticism.

> ## Using Purposeful Skepticism
>
> Take a moment to think of a politically or socially charged issue that is significant for you. What do each of the opposing sides believe? Using some critical thinking, what do you think is the truth behind this issue? Do you know your "truth" to be a fact, or is this an idea, belief, or intuition?
>
> If you think you know this as a fact, where did you get the information? What objective measures rational evidence have confirmed this? If you realize that your "truth" is actually a belief, idea, or intuition, why do you believe this? Is it based on your unique upbringing or conditioning? What has been the strongest influence in shaping this belief or idea? Is there any possibility that there may be more to this picture?
>
> How does it make you feel to employ purposeful skepticism?

The practice of purposeful skepticism is not about harsh judgment. It is about using wise discernment to get to the truth of a matter. Purposeful skepticism employs critical thinking, or what I like to call, "judicious thinking" in service of finding the truth. *Judicious* means using sensible, well-thought-out, wise judgment. It is where we bring thoughtful, organized, rational thinking in order to investigate and evaluate the connections between things. It also helps us determine what is relevant and worthwhile, and what should be discarded or put aside. With judicious thinking, we can decipher when we are being presented with facts, and when we are encountering ideas, beliefs, intuitions, fictions, falsehoods. It also helps us to assess whether the source of our information is reliable and trustworthy.

> **Exploring Judicious Thinking**
>
> Can you recall instances where judicious thinking has helped you gain deeper insight into the truth of a matter? Perhaps you have used it at work to cultivate a deeper understanding of your work environment or discover new insights about a project.
>
> Perhaps you have used it in social settings to discern the truth about a veiled social dynamic such as "gaslighting" that was playing out in a relationship.
>
> You may use judicious thinking as you wade through the daily flood of news articles – working to discern what is truthful and what might be propaganda.
>
> When we employ judicious thinking in our daily lives, we are empowered to see the truth in across our life, helping us live much more consciously and successfully.

Once we have sorted through the available information with our purposeful skepticism, we take the evidence we have found and use judicious thinking to consider the possible implications, make interpretations, and draw conclusions. We can then use our conclusions to problem solve or take productive action. Perhaps we'll find that the information causes us to rethink our initial position. We may then need to verify, test, or search for additional information so that we stand on solid ground. When we engage in this kind of mental processing, it always leads to greater success in our lives.

Purposeful skepticism and judicious thinking are cornerstones of personal and social agency. When we bring a healthy dose of skepticism and judicious thinking to our investigations of truth, we see the conditions of our world more clearly, allowing us to act more skillfully. Our brains are wonderfully designed for advanced thinking skills. They are built to be inquiring, discerning, curious, and able to detect when something is truthful or not. As we cultivate these high-level thinking skills, we begin to navigate the world with clarity and assuredness, creating a better world for ourselves and others.

# Degree of Certainty

Truth corresponds to objective reality, but can we know everything with one hundred percent certainty? We can know *some* things with one hundred percent certainty: We can be 100% certain that if we live, we die. We can know with one hundred percent certainty that change is inevitable – life changes, the world changes, and the universe is constantly changing and evolving. These are reliable truths, witnessed throughout time. Likewise, if we have a stomachache, we can be 100% certain that we have a stomachache. But for many aspects of our world, we cannot be absolutely certain that something is true. For instance, when we are suffering from a stomachache, we might believe that it is due to a meal we ate that day. But can we be completely certain that the meal is the culprit? Our stomach discomfort could be due to stress, illness, or other factors. Oftentimes, there are too many unknown variables for us to know anything definitively.

For this reason, when we are working with truth it is helpful to consider our *degree of certainty*. Our degree of certainty speaks to the percentage of how confident we are that something is true. If we have a one hundred percent degree of certainty, there is no doubt; whatever we are commenting on is absolutely true. But in most instances when talking about degree of certainty, we are not conferring an absolute quantity, for we often don't have a tool that can give us exact, objective measurements.

Instead, we are offering *impressions* – our best "guesstimate" on a subject, using our intelligence and assessment skills to calculate a measure of confidence as to how certain we are. Enlisting degrees of certainty can help us process discussions thoughtfully and make effective decisions. If the weather report says that there's a ninety percent chance that it will rain on your wedding day, you'll definitely want to make sure that you have a plan to keep yourself and your guests dry.

> Degree of certainty is meant to offer a measure of confidence in a specific truth that can help us make more thoughtful and effective decisions.

Our need for certainty depends on how high the stakes are in a given situation. If you're making dinner (and let's assume that you're not a "foodie") you may not need a high percentage of certainty regarding the exact measurement of the ingredients you're using. Making a peanut butter and jelly sandwich, you might just slather on the jelly. But if you or your guest has a severe food allergy, it is important to have a high degree of certainty about the ingredients you are using. If your friend has a peanut allergy, you need to be 100% certain that there are NO peanuts in your meal!

Oftentimes, we can't be *100% certain* about things. Even NASA (National Aeronautics and Space Administration) where they deal with extremely high stakes – flying people into space and launching important payloads – must deal with some degree of uncertainty. That is why they consciously consider and deliberately calculate degrees of certainty in all their plans.

Degrees of certainty with regard to the truth are also benchmarked in the U.S. legal system where a guarantee of freedom relies on a specific measure of certainty. When weighing legal matters of probability, the U.S. court system considers:

- *No Credible Evidence*, meaning that there are no facts substantiating the claim.
- *Some Credible Evidence*, meaning that there is some evidence worthy of being believed.
- *A Preponderance of Evidence*, which means there's a greater than fifty percent chance that something is the truth.
- *Clear and Convincing Evidence*, which means "substantially more likely than not" that something is the truth.
- *Beyond a Reasonable Doubt*, which means the degree of certainty is very strong. This is used when the stakes are very high and a person's freedom can be taken away.
- *Beyond Any Shadow of a Doubt*, which I believe is interpreted as being very close to one hundred percent certain.

I believe that a ninety percent degree of certainty is a reasonable standard of confidence when assessing if something is factual. For example, if an individual says, "I'm 90% sure he made the bank deposit yesterday," it is very likely that the bank deposit was made. While this ninety percent is still a subjective impression (it does leave open the possibility that the person speaking could be wrong), it is much more likely to be truthful than not.

Frequently, in our day-to-day life, our measurement of certainty often arises from a gut instinct – an unconscious, intuitive sense gathered from a quick integration of information held within us. In other words, we make a "guesstimate." But when the stakes are high, we need to make a more measured, thoughtful deliberation. Systematically reviewing the facts can help us get a more accurate determination and precise percentage of certainty. If we act as if we are 100% certain when all the information is not available, it can lead to chaos and disruption. Pompously announcing, "It's *definitely* not going to rain at my wedding," when weather reports say that rain is expected (even if it's sunny at the moment) can lead to a wedding disaster. When it comes to important matters, it's essential that we do not treat a moderate degree of certainty as an absolute assurance.

When utilizing degrees of certainty, it's important to have some humility. We need to hold the possibility that we could be wrong. Sometimes, despite our best efforts, as individuals and as societies, we miscalculate. But we don't need to feel ashamed about this. We can take accountability when we are wrong; we can make amends, set the record straight, and move on. With conscious, deliberate practice, we can all get more precise at conveying the truth.

# Truthful Communication

If we wish to promote truth in the world, we need to be mindful of our presence when speaking to others. When communicating, it's important to express our ideas, thoughts, beliefs, and experiences in respectful ways, making sure that we accurately describe the information concerning the topic at hand. We also want to bring an open, inquisitive mind, inviting feedback and dialogue in our exchanges. When we bring a friendly attitude, use discerning word choices, and offer clear, honest statements, we set the stage for calm, positive exchanges and skillful communication.

There are many creative ways to safeguard the truth when speaking to others. When we introduce phrases such as, "My truth is…" or "I know…" our claim should be followed up by an objective fact. We should also be mindful to not offer our beliefs, ideas, or intuitions as the truth. When talking about a *belief*, it is skillful to say, "I believe…" or "My opinion is…" If we are positing a strongly held belief, we might say, "I'm convinced that…" or "I have a powerful conviction that…" In this way, we bring clear, soothing dialogue into our exchanges – we are not riling up the room, challenging others' beliefs, or claiming that we command the *only* truth.

The same is true for our ideas. When speaking skillfully to others, we can say, "I imagine…" or "I suspect…" and then offer our idea. The same holds true for our intuitions. We might say, "My intuition is…" or "My hunch is…" And if we have a strong, powerful intuition, we can say, "I've had a deep insight…" or "My gut is telling me…" These kinds of statements clarify that we are sharing our personal beliefs, ideas, and intuitions, not positing actual truth. Speaking in this way is more precise and less controversial than saying, "Well, this is *my* truth…" or "I know for a fact that…" when it is simply a strong viewpoint.

Another way to safeguard the truth is to use the phrase, "I think…" as in, "I think Issac Newton is considered the father of modern science." "I think…" can be used anytime we refer to categories of experience (ideas, beliefs, imagination, intuition, memory, and knowledge). Other phrases also capture our personal experience: *I suppose… I surmise… It seems to me… I reckon…* Or we might declare, *My perspective is… My theory is… My hypothesis is… It seems to me that…* These expressions can always help us communicate effectively while staying true to the truth.

The next time you are in a discussion with someone, bring a warm, friendly attitude and try one of these openings. Notice if people respond more positively to your sharing. Initially, adopting these verbal devices may feel awkward, but as you practice becoming conscious of your word choices, it will begin to feel more authentic, and soon you'll see the benefits of clear communication.

I strongly believe that these simple changes in communication can decrease conflict and confusion, for we are not positing our beliefs and imaginations as truths, we are simply stating our beliefs, and it's hard to dispute what someone believes or thinks. What are they going to say… "No, you don't believe that!" "That's not your intuition!" "No, you don't think that!" It is simply what one believes; we can agree or disagree. But if we try to assert that our beliefs are *the* truth… Now that's a whole other predicament, one that can spark intense conflict and animosity.

If we want to relate to others successfully, it's also important to engage others' beliefs respectfully, even when they profess their beliefs and ideas to be "the truth." Stepping into these exchanges with kindness and curiosity, we can often soften the tension and deepen the conversation into more truthful waters. When someone posits their ideas and beliefs as statements of truth, we can simply ask, "Why do you believe that?" or

"Tell me more about your idea." Our openness and curiosity may foster more fruitful discussion and give us an opportunity to step into some clarification: "It sounds like you have some strong opinions. Where did you learn about that?" This type of communication fosters an exchange of ideas that honors different perspectives while helping us get to the truth.

When engaging others in conversation, it is also important that we manage our own emotions and reactivity. If someone challenges our deeply held beliefs, we need to calm our emotions so we can stay open to the exchange of ideas. One way to do this is to breathe out the stress and tension we are feeling in the moment, then embody a position of open curiosity. Our beliefs are *beliefs*, after all. Can we keep a relaxed posture, listen deeply, and learn from this exchange? By keeping an open mind, we may discover a new insight!

As we go through life, there will be plenty of times when we bump up against falsehoods and deceptions. If we wish to support truth on this planet, it's important that we speak to falsehoods when they are presented. In these moments, we need to be clear, assertive, sometimes, even courageous when we counter deception. During the Covid pandemic, many scientists bravely stood by their science, even as they were attacked for their findings. Ultimately, their hard work saved many lives. In speaking to the truth, we help the world become a safer, more successful place.

When addressing falsehoods in the world, we do not need to be adversarial. We can be kind, thoughtful and curious, bringing an attitude of diplomacy. With respectful, calm energy, we might say, "While I appreciate your viewpoint, I can't help but think about..." or "It's clear that this is important to you. Is this your belief, or something you know as a fact?" We can also say, "Thanks for sharing your thoughts. As I was listening, it left me with some questions. For instance, where did you get this information, is it a reliable source?"

When bumping up against others' interpretations of truth, it can also be helpful to explore their perception of truth. Sometimes, a discussion about "truth" is just what is needed. For example, we might ask, "What is your understanding of truth?" When we are inviting these conversations, it's important to stay open, calm, and curious, steering the conversation towards mutual exploration, for we all have a vested interest in discovering the truth.

When we advocate for truth respectfully and kindly, we help humanity become more successful. Today, our world is rapidly expanding: Our population is growing, and the internet allows us to communicate with more and more people, all of whom have different viewpoints and experiences. If we can learn to communicate in ways that support open, respectful dialogue and adherence to the truth, we will help secure a future that is beneficial for all.

# Final Thoughts on Truth

Our discussion of truth required some contemplation and deep thinking. Hopefully, you found the effort worthwhile and you have a deeper understanding of the complexities surrounding truth. As I said at the beginning of this book, I believe that there are few things that are as personally and socially relevant to us as the truth.

At this time in human history, the stakes are incredibly high. Our carbon use is threatening ecosystems across the earth, yet it's hard to get truthful information on this crisis. Across the internet, the truth is increasingly skewed by agitators working on their own behalf, and their messaging often creates chaos and disruption. Much of the world's wealth has shifted further away from the general populace to a smaller group of people, threatening the health and wellbeing of societies.

At the same time, we are also seeing greater distortions of the truth in the virtual world. Computer graphics allow creators to easily manipulate the truth with deep fake images and modified videos. There are countless social media influencers misrepresenting their products and information in order to boost their own sales and earnings. And importantly, Artificial Intelligence has arrived with its capacity to rewrite our world through algorithms and contrived amalgamations.

If we hope to secure a safe and equitable world in these fast-changing times, we need to make a conscious effort to seek out the truth and promote it. We need to teach our children and citizens how to seek out truth and recognize falsehoods, for we can no longer presume that the information we are getting is truthful. We need to take responsibility for addressing falsehoods and advocating for truth. Only with truth can we be accountable to what's unfolding on our planet and take the necessary steps to bring our world into balance.

To create a safer, healthier, more truthful world, we also need to address the emotional wounds and inequities on our planet, for it is our pain that causes us to manipulate the truth. When we don't feel safe, secure, or nourished, it is easy to believe that we must lie, cheat, steal, or manipulate in order to get our needs met. The more we support healing on this planet, the more we will come into alignment with truthful living.

When we tell the truth, we cannot help but be moved into action – *right action,* for we humans care deeply for each other when we are clearheaded and know the truth of the matter. And the truth of the matter is we are struggling in many areas of life: We need to tell the truth about our families, our relationships, and our communities. We need to tell the truth about what's happening on our planet. We need to tell the truth at work. And we need to tell the truth about our current economic system and its impact on the world – the truth that we cannot keep consuming and buying, for it is simply unsustainable.

When we tell the truth about our lives and the world, we will change for the better, for we will be inspired to steer our lives in a new direction. When we tell the truth about ourselves, we begin the work of healing our emotional wounds, our addictions, and our unhealthy habits. When we speak truthfully to others, we also feel less stressed. In acting honorably, there are no lies or strategies to keep track of and our mind relaxes; we sleep better, have less anxiety, and feel at ease, knowing that we are acting with integrity.

The truth also helps us resolve conflicts in our communities and around the world. When we collectively pursue truth, we better understand our world, and can't help but be moved to compassionate action. Knowing the truth, we become inspired to address the deficiencies on our planet…

create programs and education that empower our citizens… are inspired to share planetary resources… and consciously take care of our world and all the beings in it. With truth, we grow and evolve, empowering us to create a healthy, successful planet.

As we conclude this discussion on truth, let's remember the promise of a collective vision of truth. We can come together with a common goal of clarifying the truth, for a thoughtful investigation of truth will unite us in planetary wellbeing. We can recognize the importance of doing this now, at this time in history, for a collective pursuit of truth will help us right the wrongs and make decisions that will safeguard our future. If we commit to this vision – to pursue and safeguard the truth – it can be a powerful turning point in the history of humanity, putting us on a path to truly successful living.

Imagine a world where we agree to tell the truth in all areas *as best we can*. Imagine reading a newspaper, scrolling through social media, or watching a news show, knowing that the information you see is grounded in truth – it's factual and objective. Imagine sharing ideas and beliefs with others without conflict, for everyone understands the difference between truth, ideas, beliefs, and intuitions and we know how to share our viewpoints in thoughtful ways. Imagine a world where leaders tell the truth, especially in times of crisis…"We don't know all the details, but we will do our best to…" and they mean it.

If we could be assured that everyone was telling the truth to the best of their knowledge, we could *relax*, for we wouldn't need to be so vigilante. We could rest in the assurance that everyone is trying to live with integrity and uphold the well-being of all.

I encourage you to reflect on these ideas and let yourself wonder… What would a world grounded in truth look like? Might there be more ease and grace? Might we have a better chance of reaching our potential? I believe the truth will be restorative, exhilarating, and open a door to an amazing future!

# Acknowledgements

This book has come into being through the support of many wonderful people. First, I owe a huge debt of gratitude to Theresa Carson who helped craft the manuscript for this book, along with the transcripts that make up my True Success video series. Joe Vasos has been instrumental in building the vision for the videos and this book. Great thanks go to Kodii John of Medicine Sky Feather Productions who did many of the illustrations in this book. And many thanks to my sister, Kathleen Gariboldi, for her "spot-on" feedback.

I am also grateful for the love and care that my wife, Maureen, put into this book. As co-developer of True Success, she has offered great support and inspiration as I developed the manuscript for this book. With her discerning eye, she offered ideas and editing, and curated the pictures so I might offer a deeper nuance to the many ideas presented here. Without her, the vision for True Success and Truth would not get off the ground.

I have great love and appreciation for the friends and family who have supported and inspired me over the years. I am particularly grateful for Eric Larsen, Colin Smith, Jamie Knight, Louden Kiracofe, Erik Enge, Joan Cyr, Deborah Cyr, Cecilia Talamantes, Roxanne Bartel, Steve and Rose Udovich, Bolelynn Wilson, Russ Fallon, and Denis and Jane Fallon. Hours of discussion with them have sharpened my understanding of Truth and its importance in our lives.

I am also inspired by those I have studied and worked with – my professors at Stanford in my undergraduate years, my clinical supervisors at Harvard, and the many writers, researchers, and colleagues who have inspired me with their wisdom and ideas. This includes the staff and trainees at Fort Lewis College. For many years, they have given spirited feedback on my lectures about True Success and Truth.

Finally, I am thankful for the moral and emotional support I have received over the years from family, friends, and my community. I love being on this journey with my wife, and I am nourished continually by my relationships with my children, Daniel and Raven. I am held by many wonderful people in my community, as well as the Nature that surrounds my home. Living in Colorado, I am blessed to live in the mountains where I can walk, think, and ponder on the importance of Truth in our world.

## APPENDIX

# Categories of Experience as They Relate to Truth

**TRUTH**

Truth is *fact*. It is real and objective, corresponding to what actually exists. It is reliable and stable. In other words, it does not change over time. As such, we can trust it and let it guide us.

**OBJECTIVE UNIVERSAL TRUTH**

This is a truth that exists beyond an individual's knowledge or experience. It can be independently verified by anyone with the right resources.

**FALSEHOODS**

Falsehoods are the opposite of truth. They are not based on reality, and they are not objective facts. Falsehoods arise in many forms – as ignorance, confusion, mistakes, deception, lies, or delusions. Falsehoods exist both out in the world, and inside us.

## PARTIAL TRUTHS

Partial truths are real and true, but they possess only part of the whole truth. Often, the truth we see arises out of our perspective and orientation.

## THE WHOLE TRUTH

With simple issues, it is possible to hold the whole truth. For example, we can have the whole truth about whether or not it rained on us yesterday. But with complex issues, truth is often in a state of discovery and evolution – our understanding of it grows and evolves as we encounter more information. For this reason, it is often difficult to grasp the *whole* truth. As our knowledge and technology expand, we will uncover a deeper understanding of the cosmos.

## UNKNOWNS

There are many unknowns in our world. There are the things that we recognize as unknown – such as how many planets are in the universe – but there are many unknown truths that we aren't even aware of. It is important that we hold the perspective that we don't know everything.

## METAPHORS

Metaphors are figures of speech that are symbolic of something else. If your friend is really hungry, they might say, "I could eat a horse!" They are not really going to eat a horse. It is important to see metaphors for what they are and how they correspond to the truth.

## FICTION AND FANTASY

Fiction and fantasy are created out of our imagination. They may speak to truth and include truthful information, but they are not necessarily examples of truth. Fiction and fantasy can be helpful or harmful, so it is important to be mindful of the impact they have on us.

## IDEAS

Our ideas arise out of our imagination. We have ideas about the truth, but our musing may not be the actual truth. Ideas can often be checked out and tested. Ideas are great when we remember that they are simply propositions.

## CONCEPTS

Concepts are abstract ideas used to capture, group and organize information and objects into classes so we can understand and work with them. We create concepts about everything... *beauty, justice, freedom* and *love* are examples of concepts. Some concepts are truth-based, others are built on falsehoods or imaginings. Concepts are changeable. They may evolve when we find new information, or we encounter new life experiences.

## BELIEFS AND MEANINGS

A belief is a state of mind where we have placed our trust or confidence in something. Beliefs are created out of the meanings we have made about the world. Our beliefs may turn out to be the truth, but until we confirm it as objective fact, we regard it as a belief.

## INTUITIONS

Intuitions are unconscious "gut feelings." We may get powerful internal "hits" or insights, but they aren't always right because our intuitions are conditioned by our life experience. Intuitions can be important and informative but are not the same as objective truth.

## SOCIAL CONSTRUCTS

Social constructs are structured, formalized ideas created and agreed upon by people and societies to help us navigate the world. Often, they are used unconsciously, directing our social interactions, but they are not objective truth. Since they are culturally reinforced, they can be different for different people. Social constructs can help us or harm us, so we need to be conscious about using them in constructive ways.

## MIXTURES AND COMBINATIONS

All the above categories can be combined in any number of mixtures. While these mixtures of experience can be creative and useful, they can be used in harmful ways. Information often comes to us in a mixture of truths, falsehoods, fiction, beliefs, misunderstandings, or misinformation. Therefore, it is important to tease out what is truth, what is a metaphor, what is fictional fantasy, and what is deliberate manipulation.

## PERSONAL TRUTH

A term often used to describe strongly held beliefs or intuitions. People can be greatly attached to their "personal truths," so much so that they can get into fights over them. It's fine to have strong personal beliefs, but in the service of truth, it is important to remember that they are beliefs, not necessarily objective truth.

# Bibliography

Allen, Barry. *Truth in Philosophy*. Harvard University Press, 1993.

Biffle, Christopher. *A Guided Tour of Five Works by Plato: With Complete Translations of Euthyphro, Apology, Crito, Phaedo (Death Scene, and "Allegory of the Cave")*. 2nd ed., Mayfield Publishing Company, 1994. OR 3rd ed., Mayfield Publishing Company, 2000.

Blackburn, Simon. *On Truth*. Oxford University Press, 2018.

Crivelli, Pablo. *Aristotle on Truth*. Cambridge University Press, 2004.

Engel, Pascal. "Truth." *Central Problems of Philosophy*, edited by John Shand, McGill-Queens University Press, 2002.

Fallon, Kris. *Where Truth Lies: Digital Culture and Documentary Media after 9/11*. University of California Press, 2019.

Frankfurt, Harry. *On Truth*. Knopf, 2006.

Gordon, Mick, and Chris Wilkinson, (Eds.). *Conversations on Truth*. Continuum, 2009.

James, William. *The Meaning of Truth*. Prometheus, 1997.

James, William. *The Meaning of Truth: A Sequel to Pragmatism*. Ann Arbor Paperbacks, 1970.

Lynch, Michael P., Jeremy White, Junyeol Kim, and Nathan Kellen, (Eds.). *The Nature of Truth: Classic and Contemporary Perspectives*. 2nd ed., The MIT Press, 2021.

Macdonald, Hector. *Truth: How the Many Sides to Every Story Shape Our Reality*. Little, Brown Spark, 2018.

Nietzsche, Friedrich. *On Truth and Untruth: Selected Writings*. Translated and edited by Taylor Carman, Harper Perennial Modern Classics, 2010.

Orwell, George. *Orwell on Truth*. Mariner Books Classics, 2018.

Pojman, Louis P., and Lewis Vaughn. *Philosophy: The Quest for Truth*. 11th ed., Oxford University Press, 2019.

Prado, C.G. *Searle and Foucault on Truth*. Cambridge University Press, 2005.

Preyer, Gerhard, (Ed.). *Donald Davidson on Truth, Meaning, and the Mental*. Oxford University Press, 2012.

*Stanford Encyclopedia of Philosophy*. The Metaphysics Research Lab, Department of Philosophy, Stanford University, 2024, plato.stanford.edu.

Vandevelde, Pol, and Kevin Hermberg, (Eds.). *Variations on Truth: Approaches in Contemporary Phenomenology*. Continuum, 2011.

## About the Author

Mark Fallon-Cyr, M.D. is a psychiatrist who has dedicated his life to helping others live more successfully. A Harvard trained clinician, he has worked with children, adults, and families in the Four Corners region (Colorado, New Mexico, Utah, Arizona) for over 30 years, serving people from a variety of cultures and communities. For much of his career, Mark and wife, Maureen, have been developing True Success For All, a program that brings new perspectives on successful living, empowering us to realize our true potential.

www.ingramcontent.com/pod-product-compliance
Lightning Source LLC
Chambersburg PA
CBHW070640030426
42337CB00020B/4101